Praise for *Big Wild Love*

"If you're stuck in a dying or dead relationship but feel paralyzed to do anything about it, READ THIS BOOK! Epiphanies are all about taking action if you want to change your life and Jill spells out ways for you to do that, n   s out easier and faster. I wish B   n I had my 'must-leave-this-m

—**Elise Ballard**, author (*Insight to Inspire, Encourage, and Transform*

"*Big Wild Love* comes out at the perfect time: when women are rising up and realizing their own worth. Jill's book is a how to of self-reflection and self-love and lessons in how to move to a point of freedom, action, and empowerment. Anyone who has been in a bad relationship or trying to figure out if theirs is fixable should read this book."

—**Anita Busch**, journalist and victim's rights advocate

"Jill Sherer Murray takes you on the journey of letting go like your best girlfriend and pocket therapist all in one. Her fresh and candid look at relationships is full of vulnerability and heart as she teaches how to let go of the precepts—and sometimes the people—that hold us back from a big, wild love. This book will change the way you think about your life forever."

—**Jessica Rinker**, author of *Gloria Takes a Stand*, and the forthcoming *Send a Girl: The Brenda Berkman Story* and *The Dare Sisters*

"In the same way Glennon Doyle, Cheryl Strayed, and Elizabeth Gilbert lay their hearts bare, Jill Sherer Murray goes to the mat in her big, beautiful memoir come instruction manual. She teaches us not only how to let go of dead-end relationships and find the ones we long for, but offers us the tools to find and keep the most important relationship of all, that with ourselves. With wit and humor, she gives us a clear way to let go for it, embrace who we are, and invite healthy love into our lives."

—**Joy Stocke**, author of *Anatolian Days and Nights* and *Tree of Life: Turkish Home Cooking*, and former publisher of WildRiverReview.com

"Jill shares her journey towards self-love, which is unapologetically raw, real, and pure badassery. There is much to learn here for anyone who finds themselves at a painful crossroads, in need of advice on how to move forward from heartbreak."

—**Dr. Suzana Flores**, author of *Untamed: The Psychology of Marvel's Wolverine*

"*Big Wild Love* is an amazing step-by-step guide for cultivating the inner love and wisdom you need to truly let go once and for all. Jill Sherer Murray shares her own powerful story of how the lessons within led her to the true love she'd all but given up on, and so much more. A great resource and a great read!"

—**V Capaldi**, TEDx Speaker, wellness blogger

"This book is a reality check cloaked in humor, strength, and triumph. It digs into the nit and grit so many of us feel about ourselves but are afraid to say out loud. Jill does it for us, lighting the way to a better and happier place. She gives us a roadmap for seeing our worth so we can finally have the Big Wild Love we deserve."

—**Stacey Honowitz**, Supervisor Sex Crimes, TV analyst, and author

BIG WILD LOVE

BIG
WILD
LOVE

The Unstoppable
Power of Letting Go

Jill Sherer Murray

SHE WRITES PRESS

Published 2020
Printed in the United States of America
ISBN: 978-1-63152-852-1 pbk
ISBN: 978-1-63152-853-8 ebk
Library of Congress Control Number: 2019918235

For information, address:
She Writes Press
1569 Solano Ave #546
Berkeley, CA 94707

She Writes Press is a division of SparkPoint Studio, LLC.

Cover and interior design by Tabitha Lahr

All company and/or product names may be trade names, logos, trademarks, and/or registered trademarks and are the property of their respective owners.

Names and identifying characteristics have been changed to protect the privacy of certain individuals.

For the Big Wild Loves of my life:
my mom, Sandy; my dad, Owen; Hector;
and Dan, the biggest, wildest love of them all.

CONTENTS

....

INTRODUCTION

*Falling in love with yourself first doesn't make you vain
or selfish. It makes you indestructible.*

—Anonymous

There I was, sitting on a stranger's bathroom floor.
I hovered over their toilet, feeling like I had a knife in my
stomach. I rubbed my eyes while the bathroom spun around me.
I tried to hold it together . . . unsuccessfully.

The ugly cry rose from my throat like a runaway train.

I tried to console myself. I reminded myself that it was OK
to cry, that I was no Superwoman, even though, on the rare occasions on which I'd allowed myself to step out of denial, I'd thought
I could handle this. Because, if I'm to be honest, this moment of
reckoning was always something I'd anticipated and feared. Yet,
like most hard truths, I'd pushed this one so deep into my bones
I'd need a surgeon and a drill to get at it.

But here I was: curled in the fetal position on cold porcelain,
swimming in a sea of desperate thoughts, free-falling into the
deep end of disappointment.

I had asked my boyfriend, Hector, to look at a house with me that we would buy together. And just this morning, when I'd reminded him about our noon appointment, he'd said, "I'll be there." He then jostled off to the gym. I'll admit he seemed less than enthusiastic. But I didn't care. Just talking about it had been the biggest step we'd taken toward commitment in twelve years.

That is, up until he said, "I'll be there."

But little did I know that his "I'll be there" was a lie that would turn into one of my life's most defining moments.

And yet this certainly wasn't the first time Hector had promised to be somewhere for me and wasn't. Especially when I considered all the times he said he wanted to get married but wasn't ready. Or couldn't take that vacation or go to that party or visit family with me in Philadelphia because [*insert reason*].

Given all of this, I don't know why I was surprised when he promised to meet me and then didn't show up for the second time. He stood me up the first time, called to say he'd meet me later, and stood me up again.

And so there I was. Clinging to the porcelain god. My tape measure, punch list, and rose-colored glasses at the bottom of the trash basket.

Back then, Hector was my world. Sure, I had a job, friends, and a golden retriever that alleviated some of the loneliness that came from having a noncommittal boyfriend. But Hector was my beginning, middle, and end. I could stay with him, even though it was now clear he would never fully commit. Or I could leave and take the biggest risk of my life. After all, who would want a woman in her forties? Could I even start over? Could I trust again?

I slapped my hands on the cold tile in an attempt to distract myself from the pain of what was happening.

"You OK in there?" Marilyn, both the realtor and my friend, knocked on the door.

"YEP."

But I wasn't. Something powerful was happening. It was a sign from the universe, perhaps. Or just time to finally call it: admit that everything I knew about our relationship—and perhaps even my life—was over. That there was no way back to the delusion I'd artfully crafted for myself as a survival mechanism—that Hector's promise of "someday" would actually pan out.

When I showed up to look at the home at noon, I had believed in "someday." But when I got up from the bathroom floor, I knew another truth. I just didn't know if I could take that first brazen step toward a new and uncertain reality.

But then something happened, and I realized how such a first step was possible.

This thing that happened would call upon me to change everything—and find everything I wanted for myself as well.

That day, on that stranger's bathroom floor, while I was grappling with the agony of what came next, I also knew that I wasn't the first woman to struggle with whether to end a relationship with someone I loved. Countless other women have also found themselves stuck in unsatisfying relationships, feeling defeated, devalued, and desperate for something more.

Like me, they faced an impossible choice: whether to stay in a bad situation or let go, knowing that it would be a risk . . . that there were no guarantees they'd find someone else more suitable for them to love.

What I'd learned, from talking to many women over the years, was that it was a risk most people avoided. In fact, one study out of Britain showed six out of ten people would rather stay in a bad relationship, even if their partners lied, cheated, or disrespected them.[1]

The question was, why?

I surmise it's because letting go of even imperfect, unfulfilling love is hard. It requires women to have what too many just don't: the ability to be bold, take risks, and approach dating and romance with a sense of play and confidence. To use a carefully selected collection of beliefs to discern who's right for them and who isn't. And to hold out for what they really want but are afraid to ask for, in both a partner and a relationship.

And yet, while it's commonly believed that "fortune favors the bold," many women have given in to doing the opposite: engaging in excessive compromise and conceding the priorities that are most important to them—just in order to not spend the rest of their lives alone. They fear becoming cautionary tales—spinsters who lingered too long in the wrong relationships or made too many bad choices. They're settling for less, figuring that's just how it goes—part of the deal of love in the twenty-first century.

So they hold on, believing that they're worth less than what they want. For doing the opposite might be the biggest, baddest mistake of their lives. This way, they can forever prevent their ex from moving on with someone else while they wither away, alone on the vine. They never have to be faced with the prospect of meeting someone new themselves and making the same mistakes again in their next relationship.

They hold on.

Instead of letting go.

It was that fear—that fear of letting go—that kept me in an unsatisfying relationship for twelve years. And while this fear was real, I stepped onto the ledge of my life and jumped without a parachute or a net anyway. It was my only choice because I knew that, despite the pain of losing my longtime love, letting go was my way out and toward the hope and possibility I thought was long gone.

I told Hector it was over, despite his excuses for the no-shows. And then I made some long-overdue moves, which included letting go of more than just the guy. I let go of *everything*. My home in the city of Chicago, because it would have been too painful to be there without Hector. My job. My friends. My condo. I left it all to start a new life in New Hope, Pennsylvania, closer to family and where I grew up.

I had no idea that, within a year of blowing up my life, at the age of forty-two, I'd find the man who would be my husband.

Letting go has helped so many find the Big Wild Love they've always wanted—the kind they were afraid to ask for, or thought they didn't deserve, or believed was out of reach. They've learned that letting go was both the way forward to a better, happier future, and the way back to themselves.

But how does a woman truly find the boldness necessary to let go?

And what was it that I came to understand that day on the floor of the bathroom that made everything else possible?

When it comes to staying in relationships that aren't working or giving people what they want, I know that people have their reasons—I certainly had mine. I've learned this from spending decades not only dating in my own right, but also, in 2016, giving a TEDx talk about my story and how hard it was to let go of a relationship I'd known for far too long would never give me what I wanted. And the response was overwhelming.

I had no idea that those eleven minutes on the stage would spark a movement. To the contrary, I remember feeling absolutely terrified to expose so many personal truths about how I'd failed at love, in front of so many people—a live audience, a livestream audience, and then a video audience for posterity. While I was excited to share what I'd come to learn about the power of letting go and how it had changed the game for me, there was also a part of me that felt small next to the other twenty-four women who were also speaking at the event. They spoke so eloquently on big, worldly issues, like helping the poor and underserved, advocating for minorities and the rights of families, surviving and thriving in the face of diseases like cancer and multiple sclerosis. And there I was: talking about a breakup. Even though I knew it was about so much more—about what we made important in the space of our one-and-only precious life and how much we loved and valued ourselves—would the people listening get it? After all, I was there to serve them. Would they take my message of letting go and the sense of urgency I tried to convey around it to heart?

Would they use it to let go in their own lives?

The answer, to my great joy, was a resounding yes. Much to my surprise, when the talk was posted online, I started to hear from women all around the world. I had struck a chord. There was such a hunger for my insight that I not only started an advice column but also decided to write this book. And because of all of this, I now have both a researched and a firsthand account of what keeps people stuck in love.

The headlines? Most, like me, are holding onto childhood wounds that tell them that the love they want just isn't possible for them. That the devil they know is better than the devil they don't. That leaving will just offer them more heartache, so they might as well save themselves the trouble and stay where they are and simply cope their way through it.

Others don't know how to extricate themselves from a bad situation or make improvements inside a relationship that has promise, because letting go isn't always about getting rid of a relationship entirely. Sometimes, it's about brokering new agreements, especially in response to big-ticket issues like infidelity, family, sex, and money.

Many women are afraid to initiate change. They don't want to see the truth of their situations because it would be too painful. They aren't ready to take action because they don't trust themselves to make good decisions or *different* decisions. They don't see a path for going forward. Some don't even know what they want, or, if they do and it's good, they aren't sure they deserve it.

So they stay, even though they know that every day spent in a less-than-ideal situation is a sign it is time. To let go.

And yet, still, they can't see how letting the worst of love go offers them freedom: from the often-all-consuming burdens associated with coping, accepting, adapting, normalizing, and surviving inside of an untenable situation, or trying to get what they need from a nonresponsive partner.

Fortunately for me, I didn't have to suffer through this exercise for too long because that day in that stranger's bathroom led me to having a simple epiphany—I could continue to move forward with my life as it was out of love for Hector.

Or I could move forward out of love for myself.

It was either him or me.

And that day, I made my choice.

Because of the clarity I suddenly had, I knew whose life I would choose and did so.

And if all that was needed for a woman was to go out and have an epiphany, then that would be all that was necessary.

It's one thing to recognize an epiphany when it happens, but how are we supposed to move forward and actually attract it? How can we make something that's supposedly coming from our intuition more actionable? After all, it's not so easy to conjure up epiphanies since they tend to strike like lightning.

Or do they?

The fact is we have epiphanies all the time. The problem is most people sleepwalk their way through them because they're not ready to see the truth.

When my epiphany struck, I was ready to experience it—and to take action by acknowledging with a sense of finality that Hector would never, ever give me what I wanted. I'd also done more work than I'd realized in my preparations. That included creating the right conditions for epiphany by quieting my mind and opening myself up to whatever came through. By listening to and trusting my instincts and what they had to tell me. And taking steps that would culminate in such a powerful revelation when I least expected it: like imagining life without Hector, acknowledging my role and mistakes in the relationship, visualizing what it would be like on the other side of heartbreak and how I'd survive. I'd set my intention, whether I realized it or not, and in doing so, sent a clear message to the universe: it was time for that wake-up call.

Most importantly, I'd begun to examine the beliefs I held about myself and love, asking hard questions in the mirror about why I was attracted to certain types of men, why I didn't ask for more, why I stayed, and what I was getting from being stuck in a relationship going nowhere.

Allowing for that epiphany and then, ultimately, letting go, called for a lot of courage, but it also called for something else that had been missing in both my relationships and my life as a whole: self-love.

I could move forward out of love for myself by . . . actually loving myself.

Talk about epiphany.

Sadly, I'd seen many other women who didn't actively cultivate self-love, learning that no matter what their age or situation, like me, too many lacked the intimate knowledge and love of self they needed to attract healthy partners and relationships.

But what does self-love really mean in this context? By my definition, it's less about the generic "feel-good" or "pampering" kind of self-love we read about in women's magazines, and more about what I call Big Wild Love: a deliberate, intentional pursuit of taking care of oneself that allows a woman to see herself perhaps for the very first time. A process that helps us understand that at the core of who we are is a hardwired set of beliefs that can both define and derail us in love, making it hard for us to let go.

Bruce Lipton, PhD, author of *The Biology of Belief: Unleashing the Power of Consciousness, Matter, & Miracles,* says that up until the age of six, it is as if we have an internal tape recorder in our brains that is always on. And everything it sees, smells, touches, hears, or experiences in any way is being downloaded into the brain before the consciousness of the child is even made apparent.[2]

Unless we "change the tape," we then use those beliefs to make decisions through adulthood, including the choices we make in relationships.

It then follows that unless and until we consciously and deliberately go through a process of nourishing and taking care of ourselves and addressing these beliefs and how they impact us, we will lack the boldness that will empower us to let go with comfort or success.

Because it's the sense of safety we get from loving and understanding ourselves that empowers us to move forward with boldness.

Big Wild Love enables us to take the risks that will change our lives.

This is what *Big Wild Love* is all about. In it, I'll take you through the process I used to love and understand myself and let go for a better life.

Because it's only when people truly let go that they can realize what's possible.

In this book, you'll find a practical, alarmingly simple, step-by-step framework for helping you find your own Big Wild Love. It is a guide you can use to understand the art and practice of letting go so as to rid yourself of a life and love that aren't working. It will empower you to find a life and love that do.

I'll show you the value of Big Wild Love and help you to cultivate it so you can move boldly through the most critical transitions of your life. I'll take you through the six steps I used to get from a life and half-love that fell short to one that gave me everything I wanted and more. This includes recognizing the epiphany, feeling in the aftermath, identifying the end goal, navigating the options for getting there, creating a letting-go hit list, and pulling it all together into a documented, comprehensive, and actionable plan that will not only keep you on track but also hold you accountable on the promises you've made to yourself.

This book will show you that no matter where you are in the process, you are not alone. Each chapter is anchored by a story from my own life for context, followed up by research, insights, and stories of other women to show you just how accessible each step is.

If you're struggling in an unfulfilling relationship, you may falsely believe that because you're stuck now, that will always be the case. But this just isn't true. This book will show you how to let go so you can welcome a new beginning back into your life and reclaim the self you've lost.

Big Wild Love will show you why you should give yourself a chance at the healthy, joyful love you deserve. My experience as well as the experiences of so many other women demonstrates that it is indeed possible.

Big Wild Love is for you. It will give you a process for going from your own respective "floor" to being happily ensconced in a relationship with another person. It will also help you find the most important love story of them all: the one you want with yourself.

Part One:

BIG
WILD
LOVE

Chapter 1

SELF-LOVE WITH INTENTION

I was in a long-term relationship where marriage was just out of reach. I left him four years ago, at age forty-two, thinking I'd find someone else quickly. It didn't happen. And I've been OBSESSED . . . with finding new love, weeping buckets of tears, and pleading with God for help. Then I saw your TEDx talk and decided that enough is enough. My goal, for now, is to LET GO of trying to find love with another person and love the hell out of myself instead.

—Josie, 46, New York City

I had no idea when I walked into a bar with friends on a random Friday night that my life would change. But it did. Because that's where I would meet Hector. Sweet, kind, loving, generous, and charismatic Hector.

I was drinking coffee at the bar, feeling bored, when he came up behind me and ordered the same.

"You're drinking coffee too?" he asked, as his dark eyes pierced mine.

"Oh, yeah." I smiled. He was cute alright.

"Would you like some more?" He motioned to the bartender.

"Are you trying to get me drunk?" I asked.

"More like heart palps."

Mission accomplished, I thought.

He was there with friends, leaving for a two-week vacation the next day. After talking for hours, he took my number and vowed to call when he got back. I was pretty sure I'd never hear from him again. But much to my surprise, he called two weeks to the day.

We met for dinner in Greektown. I'd forgotten how adorable he was: dark curly hair, olive-toned skin, perfectly aligned features. Smart and interesting, he opened doors, held chairs, paid for dinner, and loved his mother. A real gentleman, he was genuinely surprised when I kissed him at the end of our date while we waited for the valet. I was surprised too. And yet I felt compelled to press my lips against his; doing so left me in full tilt the entire drive home. He was the whole package.

I remember asking myself how I'd stumbled upon such a Kim Kardashian diamond. I even allowed myself to wonder whether he could be "the one."

As it turned out, he would be: the one to teach me what it meant to be good. And that I deserved to be loved. He would also be the one to teach me how, ultimately, to love myself.

Because I didn't love myself going in, as evidenced by the failed relationships I'd had before him. I can see now where a lack of self-love inspired me to make less-than-ideal choices. But back then, I blamed them on either the men being cads or on me being naïve. I even considered the idea that maybe I was destined to be alone.

Self-love wasn't even on my radar. Nobody ever taught me it mattered. To the contrary, I'd learned that winning the love of *another* person was the prize. That I should do whatever it took to get it, even if it meant sacrificing myself. Which I did with great energy. After all, it took me ten years of being with Hector to confess to him that I wanted marriage—something I'd lied about for fear of turning him off.

While I knew he didn't want the same from the start, I'd secretly hoped he'd change his mind. It would take me another two years to acquiesce that he wouldn't, even if I waited long enough. Or if I got prettier, thinner, or more lovable.

Instead of hoping for more, I decided I'd work on seeing the value in less. I had accepted what was: a loving relationship on his terms. Whenever I'd question whether that was best for me, I'd remind myself that marriage was just a scrap of paper.

It was a negotiation I'd have with myself over and over, until a dying friend of both mine and Hector's woke me up to a larger truth.

"I love you and Hector . . ." she began.

"We love you too, Mari." I tried not to cry. Fucking cancer.

"I'm not doing well, so I'm not gonna mince words . . ."

I could feel my heart drop. I had no clue what was coming next.

"He loves you but will never give you what you want, *mija*. He doesn't want it. He told me."

Hector was indeed sweet, kind, loving, generous, and charismatic.

But as it turned out, he was also unavailable.

Suddenly I felt dizzy.

"You're forty and living alone. Don't be alone at fifty. Go find him—the one who will give you what you deserve."

I guessed that since she couldn't save her own life, perhaps she was trying to save mine.

Her words haunted me. They gave me the courage to push the limits by suggesting that Hector and I see that house. And I felt her like an angel on my shoulder while I was breaking down in that stranger's bathroom, finally asking *the* question: why was I holding on so tightly?

It was one I couldn't bring myself to ask earlier, when I was terrified of losing someone whose only crime was not wanting what I did. Maybe if he'd been more like the others—disrespectful, cold, and withholding—the decision to let go would have been easier.

But now the floodgates were open.

What would happen to me if I let go? Would I be alone forever? What would I do with the shame, anger, and self-loathing I'd felt for betraying myself? How would I move forward?

I'd ask these questions and others until there were none left to ask. I didn't have the answers, but I was ready to find them. And that made me feel oddly safe. Like no matter what happened, I'd be OK.

Hector may have been the one to teach me that I deserved to be loved and how to love myself. But it wasn't because he was the perfect boyfriend or because I stayed with him.

It was because, in the end, I found out what the issue really was.

Simple, but Not Easy

When I gave my TEDx talk, I had no idea that it would resonate with so many people around the single unifying issue that we're staying too long in relationships that do not serve. I continue to see this play out every day in the e-mails I receive from women (and, by the way, men) struggling to find themselves in love.

Like Christine, who stayed with her husband for twenty-three years to keep her family together, even though her marriage had unraveled years earlier when he traveled every week for business and left her to raise their children alone.

Or Terri, who stayed with her husband for three years, despite the fact that she was in love with a woman, because she was afraid her family and her church would never accept her as a lesbian.

Then there was Joan, who stayed with her boyfriend for four years before accepting that she'd never be as important to him as his business.

And Sandy, who clung to the boyfriend she'd met on vacation. He called her his "soul mate" but then turned cold after the holiday and said he needed to get "back to reality."

In these examples and many others, each of these people had a choice. They could stay in the relationship—or tethered to the idea of it—and the belief that it might just be their only chance at love. Or they could let go.

It's a choice we all have when faced with a crossroads. We can hold on to a relationship that's not giving us what we want, knowing that we're agreeing to keep ourselves stuck.

Or we can let go and give ourselves a real chance at finding the healthy love we really want.

That's it.

Simple, but certainly not easy.

Most people, especially those who don't love themselves, will invariably choose to hold on to the relationship, avoiding the act of letting go at almost all costs. And those costs can be steep, including time, freedom, peace of mind, safety, the opportunity to meet the real love of their lives, morals, and even better health. For example, did you know that you are 35 percent more likely to become ill if you're in an unhappy relationship?[3]

Makes sense if you consider that it's often our bodies that

slow us down when we're burning the candle at both ends, giving over too much of ourselves to other people.

"We get sick because we forget to take care of ourselves when the world around us says, 'Do for me,'" says author, psychologist, and healer Susan Barbara Apollon. "And yet doing for ourselves is why we're really here. If I'm in a situation that's not good for me, I need to pause, go inside, and explore why. I need to learn how to love myself better so I can be here most joyfully, which might mean saying 'thanks but no thanks' to somebody else."

And yet too many don't do that. Instead they hold on to relationships that aren't good for them because it's too daunting to walk away. They don't want to go through what I call the "Tunnel of Pain" (more on this later), or worse, being alone. They're not ready to delve inward, to push past fear and insecurity on the chance that there'll be something better waiting for them on the other side.

Staying stuck seems like a gentler option despite promising more of the same: the sense of fighting an uphill battle all the time. Of feeling less than valued. The fear of leaving, speaking up for what they want, or asking for more. The need to over-compromise, or please others at the expense of themselves. A curiosity around other people's relationships, imagining they're better than their own. Uncertainty whether the situation they're in is right for them, needing constant input and reassurance.

I'm not saying that all relationships are perfect all the time or that even the best of them don't require work or encounter challenges. But most people in healthy situations don't walk around daydreaming about what it would be like to be anywhere else with anybody else.

This is what happens when you don't love yourself enough to take a chance on what's possible. I know. And it sucks.

Still, the fact remains: without self-love, you'll never really feel sure about when or whether to walk away. You'll always take whatever someone has to give, even if it's not enough (and it usually isn't). You'll never believe that you deserve much or rock the boat to get it. You'll be stressed by an overzealousness to please and a dependence on other people for happiness and validation. And while you'll tire of your partner's bad behavior, you'll also find yourself frustrated by not being able to share your true feelings. All at the expense of real intimacy. And the stories you tell yourself about what you deserve from love? Forget about it.

"For a long time, I had to let go of the idea that I was unlovable," says Denise, who's been married to her high school sweetheart for eighteen years. She says her lack of self-worth was a problem over the years, creating conflict in her marriage. "It stood in the way of receiving the love I didn't think I deserved. Doubt, fear, skepticism, cynicism, paranoia, you name it, I was hardwired for it. Always waiting for the other shoe to drop affected everything."

Instead of letting go, people who lack self-love do what I did for all of those years with Hector: They cling to their relationship, sabotaging their efforts at healthy love by making choices to their detriment and failing to break destructive patterns. They spend their time looking for answers in other people, failing to explore who they are. These thoughts derail not only their efforts but also what they really want from love. As a result, they take whatever they can get without discretion, keeping themselves stuck, unless and until it simply becomes too unbearable (if they ever get there) and they decide to give up on love altogether.

Big Wild Love Is Key

As I said at the beginning of the chapter, I learned from my time with Hector that I deserved to be loved. I was ultimately able to do this because I came to understand that the issue wasn't that he and all the other men were immature or cads or something else, but because I didn't love myself.

And this is what people who are in a similar position can understand for themselves.

Remember how I said that people who don't love themselves avoid letting go like the plague? Well, people who *do* love themselves let go often. That's because they look for answers inside of themselves. They know who they are and what they want from love. They have a surety about what needs to come next, even if it's hard or it hurts, or they don't know what's waiting around the bend or how it will all turn out. Like leaving a relationship that's just not working. Stepping back into the dating fray, trusting themselves to know they're ready to attract healthy suitors and to make healthy decisions. Asking for what they want or need from a partner who has promise.

People who love themselves know that they always have choices, and they don't attach to one "right" path. They know that no matter what the consequences, they're not going to settle for less than they want or deserve. And that despite whatever happens, they'll always be OK.

They believe they will be OK, and therefore they will be. And they believe this because they love themselves.

And this becomes the entryway to a bigger and better life.

The people I'm talking about are practicing a kind of self-love that's different from the more generic version. The kind that promotes, for example, eating healthy foods, making time for exercise, going for a massage or a new hobby, taking a long walk, and spending time with treasured friends and community. This "feel-good" type is more about self-care than self-love. It advocates for activities that help you feel good from the outside in.

And believe me. I get it. These are all great things to do, and I would never recommend you avoid them.

But they're also not enough to build and sustain the foundation we need to act boldly when situations call for it or take the appropriate risks to let go for what we want. To do that, we need to radically shift how we think about loving ourselves by flipping this traditional approach on its head: instead of having us bring elements from the *outside in*, the brand of self-love I'm talking about has us work from the *inside out*. This may not always feel as good as self-care, but it moves us closer to the lives and love we're after.

After letting go of Hector, I spent many nights out with friends, getting massages, and reading magazines about how to use self-care techniques to move on from heartbreak. But I more profoundly moved myself forward by engaging in self-exploration, going inward to understand who I was, and uncovering what I believed about myself and love. I cultivated my version of the "Big Wild Love" (or BWL) I needed to let go for what I wanted—including a new, carefully curated relationship and life—over and over again.

This is how it happened for me.

And the good news is it can happen this way for you when you practice BWL yourself.

BWL will have you take the more generic approach to a deeper place by adding intention. Namely, to love and understand the basics of who you are and what moves you, so you can (a) find the courage and confidence to make the big and often scary moves, and (b) create the sense of safety and empowerment you need to take the risks associated with letting go.

Because it is, in fact, this sense of safety we get from understanding and loving ourselves that empowers us to move forward with boldness.

It empowers us to take risks.

After all, letting go for the things we want in life involves a great deal of risk—sometimes the biggest of our lives. And yet if you're not uncomfortable while doing it, chances are you're not letting go properly but rather accepting, normalizing, coping, or giving up on getting what you need from a relationship instead. Which may feel easier in the moment but won't advance your cause or get you to a better place in the long term.

Just ask Maxine, a forty-two-year-old yoga instructor who was raised by an alcoholic father and a passive mother who promised to leave her father but never did. At the age of ten, Maxine began begging her mother to go, until she herself left home at seventeen to marry her first alcoholic husband. There'd be two more right behind him. She'd marry and leave them all to prove to her mother: *This is how it's done.* She may have been leaving or giving up on her partners, but she wasn't letting go of the childhood wounds that had her making the same mistakes over and over . . . and over.

It was only when Maxine started doing the work to love and understand herself that she was ready to find healthy love. And she did. But she had to let go of the old *stuff* to get there. And so, too, do you.

BWL allows you to find love with another person by finding love for yourself first. It's a get-out-of-jail-free card from needless suffering. After cultivating my own BWL, I went from feeling trapped to deciding that no matter what happened—whether I found someone else after Hector or I didn't—I'd still be happy. It taught me to stop looking outside of myself for that happiness.

"When I first got sick, I had to figure out what really made me happy," says V., a fifty-six-year-old community health advocate and blogger whose husband left her when she was told her multiple sclerosis had progressed to the most advanced stage. "I learned that a lot of what I was basing my life decisions on [were] things I didn't believe. I felt like a fraud. In order to become the person I am now, I had to face hard truths and let go of the person I was. I reinvented myself by loving myself first and foremost."

At first, V. did what she could to take care of herself with gentle exercise, a special diet, and going on "self-love" dates to the museum. Her condition required some of those things, but when she set out to practice Big Wild Love, she began peeling back the very layers of who she was. That meant questioning the core values she'd held for most of her life, from her traditional Italian upbringing and conditioning as a successful business-woman (she'd earned her first million by age thirty), to her sexuality. Then she asked herself what truly made her happy and thriving. And what changes she needed to make to go from the woman she was to the woman she wanted to be.

Big Wild Love gives you permission to explore—the gift of introspection, taking you off the path of what you don't want and pointing you in the direction of what you do. It will give you the courage to let go, allowing you to recognize and address blind spots or triggers before they derail your efforts, simply because you know doing so is what's best for you—and you care about that. Big time.

Big Wild Love will attract other big wild loving people to you and keep you focused on your own issues. You will be able to address those issues without wasting time trying to figure out somebody else's motivation. BWL will never ask you to be perfect. To the contrary, it will show you that vulnerability is strength. And that the best of love is about bringing the best *version* of yourself to the table *and* wanting the best for yourself.

Because you finally believe you're worth it.

"Once you come from a self-loving heart, all things are possible," V. says. "Fear and worry leave, along with everything that makes love with another person so tortured. I didn't know what love was until I understood what self-love meant for me. Then love became like a trampoline. I'd jump up and down, and it would always be under my feet."

Through the Tunnel to the Light

So now that you know what BWL is and why it's so important, how do you get it? Aha! The answer is by taking a trip through the Tunnel of Pain (TOP) I mentioned earlier.

If you've ever suffered the ruins of love, you know this tunnel well. It's essentially where we go to feel the scalding hot burn of what and *who* just happened to us. To say it's not fun is an understatement, which is why we avoid it like the orthodontist.

The sureties? It will be dark, and we'll be alone. There will be unnerving silence and the stench of sewer and mud. The bats and birds of our imagination will eat and peck away at us with all kinds of destructive thoughts—about ourselves, our destiny, our worth, and every injustice that's ever been done to us since birth.

As we search frantically for the exit, we will swing from one mood to the next. Walk in circles. Forget to eat, sleep, or smile. Even when we're forced out into the world with other people, we'll remain lost in the rough and tumble of our own thoughts, certain we will never feel better. Never be found. Never be understood. We'll question not only whether we'll make it to the light but whether the light actually exists.

The TOP called to me like a howling, angry coyote for years before I could muster the courage to get close. Until I had that epiphany in that stranger's bathroom and realized that if I ever wanted to find the love I was starting to believe might not be possible, I'd have to take that first bold step inside. That meant believing (a) the light *did* exist, (b) the love I wanted was possible, and (c) I deserved it.

Getting to the other side meant I actually had to believe in myself. That brought forth a new epiphany: BWL *was* the light. And it is for you too. Because it's only when you know how to love yourself with an open mind and heart, and in celebration of who you are, that you can love other people in kind.

Which begs the question: How do you get there? By preparing yourself to take that trek and get the most out of it. And that requires the following:

Feel bad. OK, so I think you get by now that the TOP is not a five-star resort. At the same time, it's important to recognize that the pain exists for a purpose—to remind you of what you don't want and to serve you in getting what you do. Because shivering in the dark forces you to not only rely on but also *understand* the deepest parts of yourself as a way to get through it. As a result, you'll learn a few things about who you are that you wouldn't otherwise. It's like going on an archeological dig of your own psyche.

As you do, I warn you: you might find some things you don't like, and that's not only OK, it's the point. Remember the goal is not judgment but going beyond your everyday consciousness, to know yourself so you can make the internal changes needed to get the love and relationship you want on the next go-around. Feeling bad is all about introspection, actualization, and ultimately, reclamation on your own terms.

To get there, you'll need to pay attention to your thoughts and what they're telling you about who you are, using the same hyperawareness you'd have if you were actually trapped and desperate to find your way to safety. Because for all intents and purposes, you are. And the stakes are high. After all, this business of love—and believing that you're lovable—has broad ramifications for your life. Outdated thoughts and beliefs that linger below the surface have the power to keep you stuck for as long as you let them. We'll talk more about this in the next chapter.

Accept what's real. That means making peace with the reality of your situation. Coming out of any denial that there is hope for a relationship gone wrong when either you or the other person has made it clear there isn't. All too often, we deny what's right in front of us and hold on to a picture of a life that we hoped would have happened for far too long, until we realize it won't and that there is nothing to be salvaged by staying.

Accepting what's real also means that you understand the difference between the longer-term strategy of letting go and shorter-term strategies designed to help you survive, like accepting, normalizing, giving up, or coping inside of a relationship. These approaches may make you feel better or safer in the moment, but they won't ultimately get you where you want to go. The only way to do that is to be brutally honest with yourself about what's really going on and fully let go of whatever is standing in between you and the desired outcome. That means seeing the possibilities and *probabilities* for what they are, asking yourself two very important questions: Do you feel it's possible to save your current relationship or that things will change in your favor? And then, keeping in mind that anything is possible, asking yourself if it's *probable*. Journal around the answer for more insights.

Take an honest account of your mistakes. It's only natural to conduct a postmortem after a relationship ends. As you do, remember that it takes two to tango, and no one person is ever fully to blame. And that's OK! Healthy relationships can withstand error. (A dear friend once said to me, as I was lamenting about something I'd said to a boyfriend, fearful I'd put him off: "If it's that fragile, is it really worth it?" I never forgot her words.) What's more important than beating yourself up for these errors is to own yours in particular—and not waste time spinning on mistakes made by other people. That's not your work, it's theirs. Instead, take your lessons so you don't repeat them the next time, knowing that every failed step out of the gate has something to teach you about who you are, what you want, and as importantly, what you don't.

Once you acknowledge your mistakes, take yourself off the hook for them. As you evolve toward greater BWL, you'll come to see that beating yourself up for what you didn't know or for being imperfect is a waste of time and energy. Forgiving yourself will free you not only to give and receive love without harboring any negative residual feelings from a previous relationship, but to help you forgive others as well.

"Part of finding the power to love ourselves involves being kind enough to forgive ourselves for anything and everything we've done that we view as not being good for either ourselves or other people," says Apollon. "That means letting go of guilt. Saying 'I forgive me because I love me,' that's what unconditional love is."

Finally, give yourself the time and space you need to grieve the loss of love. Because whether you called it off or your partner did, you'll need time to experience your emotions around losing a life you had or thought you'd have and the heaviness you feel knowing it's gone or won't happen. Unless you do, you won't be able to heal, which is the only way to restore wholeness and balance physically and emotionally. Allow yourself to "cut the cords," as Apollon says, to anyone or anything that belongs to your past. Focus on what makes you happy when you look out the window and know that it's all there, waiting for you when you're ready.

Believe that you are worthy. Repeat after me: *You are good enough. You are good enough. You are!* Know it in the face of good loving times and bad. When someone tries to tell you otherwise. In the choices that you make. By never begging for what or who doesn't want to stay, especially when that someone is showing signs of apathy or downright disinterest. As a Big Wild Loving person, know you always deserve more.

Remember that while you don't need to beg for love, you also don't need to be perfect to have it, which is impossible anyway. Nobody is perfect. You have a 100 percent failure rate here. Instead, you're looking to be with someone who accepts you for all that you are. Start by accepting yourself first.

Inherent in knowing that you deserve healthy love—where two people are equally invested in the relationship, compromising, and committed to loving and honoring one another—is trusting your instincts. Because you believe what they're telling you. After all, we have them for a reason—to alert us when there is danger and to keep us safe from it. As part of that, it's also important to listen to your own voice above all others, especially when it comes to matters of the heart. You do know best. You have the answers, you just don't always listen to what your gut is telling you, letting other people's voices and expectations create doubt and override what you know to be true. Instead, let your own desires, thoughts, and ideas dictate your actions and beliefs about yourself.

Know that no matter what happens, you'll be OK. This is really where the rubber of BWL hits the road, because it keeps you grounded in the fact that you will be OK, no matter what: because you've got *you.* When I let go of Hector and was going through the tunnel, I came to learn that unless and until I could be happy on my own—by loving, understanding, and trusting myself—I might never make the right, best decisions in love. Instead, fear and desperation would become my North Star. I had to learn, just like you do, that to get the love we want, we have to let go of the idea that it's promised, that it will show up when we want it, and most importantly, that we need it to be whole. We don't. We can choose to be whole on our own whenever we want by making ourselves the very best loves of our lives. The funny thing is that once we truly believe and feel that, love with another person comes. When we least expect it. You've heard that, yes? Truth bomb.

As you move through the TOP, remember to get help if you need it. After all, even the best spelunkers in the world need the right tools and guides to help them navigate tricky terrain. I believe asking for help is the true meaning of life (along with having good credit). Strong, Big Wild Loving people do this. Be one of them.

Lastly, know that as you make your way through the tunnel, you may be tempted to turn around at some point. Because it's hard. Resist, please. While the pull for relief may be strong—and you may want to revert back to that generic version of self-love to distract yourself—stay focused. Engage in self-care, sure. But don't let it replace the work you're doing in the darkness. Stay the course until you're done. Keep your eyes forward and your feet moving. Promise yourself that you'll go the distance. That you'll allow yourself to feel every lump, bump, and scrape in that tunnel until you've hit the buried treasure inside of yourself—the gold that will give you the answers you need to finally win at love.

This is how BWL happens. And once you've got it, it will also be there to ground you and to give you the sense of safety you need to act boldly and let go for the right kind of love.

Two-Day Relationship Detox: A Plan for BWL

Now that I've gone over the five ways to begin cultivating Big Wild Love, here's a great way to get started putting these principles into action. If you're in a relationship and not sure where you want things to go, this two-day relationship detox will yield important insights that will help you in deciding whether to stay and work things out, or fully let go.

Day One will call upon you to continue cultivating BWL by engaging in the generic self-love, pampering yourself, and feeling good. That's because self-care and self-love are extremely synchronous in the context of this experience, as you'll soon find out. It's also about unwinding, embracing the quiet, taking space away from the day-to-day grind, and *listening* to create the optimal conditions for epiphany, which will offer you the truth and clarity you need to move forward.

On Day Two, you'll go deeper, asking and answering questions you may have never addressed before or thought about in the same way you will after gaining the clarity that comes from a day of self-care and distance from daily life.

Plan to do the detox when you have a forty-eight-hour block of time, which you may need to carve out with intention. Then, for the detox to be most powerful, find your way to neutral ground (e.g., rent an Airbnb or house-sit for a friend) since new surroundings often lead to important new insights.

You also want to bring provisions, including a journal or notebook, comfortable clothes for relaxing and light exercise, a good read or art supplies, or whatever will help you relax. I'd also bring a bag of healthy groceries because eating a healthy diet (while a glass or two of wine at night may be fine, leave the Oreos and soda at home) will give you the energy and focus you need to use this time most productively.

Once you're ready to get started, consider that the detox is already organized for you and well-timed; the schedule assumes that you'll be at your destination at the start and not still traveling to it. Plan to spend the time alone and uninterrupted. Let friends, family, and anybody else who may look for you know that unless there's an emergency, you'll be unavailable. Lastly, consider the schedule a blueprint for how to spend the time, but feel free to find pacing that feels right for you.

OK, ready to get started? I'm excited for you. Here you go:

Day One

8:00 a.m. Do three pages of longhand, stream-of-consciousness writing. Don't worry about grammar or it being good. Just keep your hand moving on the page, putting down anything and everything that crosses your mind—for your eyes only. The goal is to provoke, clarify, comfort, cajole, prioritize, and synchronize the day at hand. Don't overthink it.

8:45 a.m. Have a healthy breakfast, or whatever is your morning ritual, and prepare for the day.

10:00 a.m. Meditate.

10:30 a.m. Go for a gentle walk, do yoga, stretch, or perform some other light form of exercise.

12:00 p.m. Make yourself lunch. Take the time to make real food instead of using convenience food.

1:00 p.m. Enjoy reading or television, anything you'd like as long as it doesn't stress you out or take you too far away from your thoughts.

2:00 p.m. Relax, breathe, and *process*. Do whatever helps you get grounded in your feelings. Read *People* magazine, create a vision board, sketch, write, cry (sometimes when we're finally still, we get very emotional), or watch your favorite TEDx talk. :) Sink into thinking about where you are in your relationship and life and see what arises. Let your mind wander.

5:00 p.m. Nap (no longer than twenty minutes).

5:20 p.m. Free time to relax until dinner. Take a hot bath, read, sit in nature and listen. Do not catch up on work, check e-mail or voicemail, or watch stressful television.

6:00 p.m. Repeat lunch ritual for dinner.

7:00 p.m. Get quiet, again. Listen to calm music or just sit and breathe. I know there's a lot of this in Day One, but we spend a lot of time filling every second of our lives. It's important to just be—especially if we want our minds to bring us new ideas!

8:00 p.m. Journal more deliberately than you did in the morning around how the day went and anything you learned. Then write the following questions on a page in your notebook in preparation for tomorrow's journal entry.

- What do I want from love?
- Am I getting it? Why or why not?
- What does a happy relationship look like, and how do I feel inside of it?
- Do I believe it's possible for me?

9:00 p.m. Go to bed. You may be tired since dealing with your inner world can be mentally and even physically exhausting!

Day Two

8:00 a.m. Wake up and answer the questions you wrote in your notebook before you went to bed. If you need more than three pages, that's OK. Just don't spend more than the allotted time. Make coffee first if you must, but quickly. You want to get that pen to paper as close to waking time as possible.

8:45 a.m. Have a healthy breakfast, or whatever is your morning ritual, and prepare for the day.

9:15 a.m. Go for a gentle walk, do yoga, stretch, or perform some other light form of exercise.

Please note: As you move into Day Two, take the full time allotted to complete each section since the material is designed to provoke thought, questions, and internal dialogue. If you're moving through too quickly, you're *not* doing the inner work required to get results. Don't shortchange yourself. Instead, go beyond the surface for answers and really challenge yourself to go deep. And if you're not sure how or you get stuck, here are some suggestions:

- Go for a short walk.
- Take a break. (Totally OK to do this if you need it!)
- Do a short meditation on the specific thought/concept/ idea that has you at a standstill.
- Journal it out.
- Talk it through while "tapping," or using Emotional Freedom Techniques, which is one of my favorite ways to de-stress and get new insights on my own feelings (www. thetappingsolution.com).
- Reverse the question or prompt to get another perspective (e.g., "What *do* you want from love/relationship?" to "What *don't* you want from love/relationship?," etc.).
- Respond to each question or prompt as if you're doing them as morning pages—just keep your hand moving on the page and let your subconscious take over. The answers will come!
- Remember, this is for your eyes only, so don't let the thought of sharing with other people get in your way or derail your vulnerability.

10:00 a.m. Take out your notebook and respond to these questions and prompts:

1. Finish these sentences:
    - I had no idea that I believed _____ about myself.
    - I had no idea that I believed _____ about my relationship.
    - I believe that I deserve _____ from my partner and I don't deserve _____ from my partner.

2. Did you have any (general or relationship-related) epiphanies or revelations over the past twenty-four hours?
3. If yes, what where they and what did you learn from them?
4. What do you want from love and a relationship? What does that look like for you?
5. Do you have those things in your current situation?
6. Why or why not?
7. What's the real problem in your situation and whose is it—yours, your partner's, or yours to share as a couple?
8. Do you think it's solvable?
   - If yes, what do you think are some potential solutions?
   - If not, what are your options? How about in the context of what you ultimately want from love?

12:00 p.m. Make and enjoy a nourishing lunch, as you did yesterday. Take a break.

1:00 p.m. Go back to your notebook and respond to these questions and prompts:

9. What beliefs do you have about yourself and who you are in love that you think may be holding you back from what you want, contributing to the struggle in your current situation, or sabotaging your efforts?
10. Finish these sentences:
    - I hold on because I get _____ from being in this relationship and with this person.
    - I would feel very _____ if I held on to this relationship after this detox.
    - If I hold on to this relationship, then _____.

- I want to let go because I don't get _____ from being in this relationship and with this person.
- I would feel very _____ by letting go of the relationship.
- If I let go of this relationship, then _____ .

11. Make a one-paragraph case for holding on and then a one-paragraph case for letting go.
12. If there were no other voices in your head but your own, and you were just going on *your* pure instinct, what would it tell you to do?

As you move through these exercises, allow yourself to write in a free-form way around each prompt. You may start by responding to the initial query, but if you find it takes you somewhere else, go with it. Sometimes that's where the magic happens. And if you need, remember to include the prompt about possibility versus probability, as I mentioned earlier.

Feel free to journal specifically around each of the five methods for cultivating BWL (e.g., feel bad, accept what's real, take an honest account of your mistakes, believe that you are worthy, and know that no matter what happens, you'll be OK). If you don't have enough time during this day, do it as homework. Start by writing one paragraph around the following questions to jog your thinking and any epiphanies. You'll find these are good questions to ask yourself over and over again, as you go through life learning how to evaluate what's best for you, taking the risks you need to take to let go as a practice:

13. How do I feel about feeling bad? Do I tend to avoid it or am I more likely to dive in, knowing it will ultimately lead me to a better place?

14. Am I someone who is unwilling to see things for what they truly are, or am I more inclined to accept reality? How does that work for me? (For example, I tend to be calm in a tough situation or emergency. But once it's sunk in, I can get emotional. Knowing this, I don't beat myself up for it but rather work my way through it gently and with self-compassion. How about you?)

15. Is it difficult for me to accept that I've made a mistake? Do I beat myself up for it rather than learning from it?

16. Whose voice, other than my own, do I most hear in my head?

17. Am I open to the idea that I don't always do things to perfection and willing to accept constructive feedback?

18. What do I believe about myself that I may not have written down in the earlier prompt, after responding to the other questions?

19. Do I fear that I won't be OK if I take a risk? Or if the person I'm with leaves me? What is that fear about, and where does it come from?

20. Do I worry about taking care of myself? Or am I the kind of person who tends to believe that it'll all work out?

3:00 p.m. Nap (fifteen minutes).

3:15 p.m. Go for a gentle walk, do yoga, stretch, or perform some other light form of exercise.

4:00 p.m. Begin pulling together what you've learned into a rough and high-level plan based on the above. Include the following:

21. What was the moment that helped you to see what you needed to do more clearly?

22. How do you feel about this revelation? Write about the good, the bad, and the ugly! Don't hold back.

23. What do you want from love and a relationship? Be honest. Once you've decided on what you want . . .

24. Identify your options for getting there. Remember, there are many ways to get where you want to go. Decide which option you'll take to get to your desired outcome.

25. Whether you've decided to hold on or let go, there are things you'll need to let go of to do so effectively (e.g., limiting beliefs about yourself or your partner, expectations, thoughts, rules, outcomes, etc.). What are they? And then which, specifically, do you need to work on to achieve your end goal through the desired option? Lay them out. Begin to identify *how* you'll work on letting them go (e.g., counseling, morning writing, leaning on friends and family members for support, classes, yoga, meditation, Emotional Freedom Technique, etc.).

26. Cull from each of these answers your beginning action steps. Lay them out as follows:
    - Where I'm going
    - How I'm getting there
    - What I'm letting go of to make sure I'm successful
    - Tasks/timing
    - Anything else you think you need to begin to flesh out this plan further or put it into action!

6 p.m. Dinner (as you did lunch).

8 p.m. Relax, watch TV, read a book, listen to music, or head back home.

As I said earlier, if you run out of time, keep going once you get home and the detox is "officially" over. It doesn't mean self-exploration has to end. I like to ask and answer some of these questions periodically as life challenges surface, either in the morning or just after exercise, because I'm more tired and less likely to resist what comes up.

I also encourage you to ask yourself how it felt to be alone for two days and whether you could do it again. After all, you don't need an invitation to take space for introspection and problem-solving. Big wild loving people know when they need to rest, explore, and rejuvenate.

Then keep going on your plan, incorporating each step as outlined at the end of Day Two. Make your morning writing practice a ritual, along with letting go, to stay connected to yourself and practice Big Wild Love.

Happy on My Own

As I moved through my own journey in cultivating this important skill, I realized a lot of things that continue to serve me to this day.

I recognized that, while I didn't want to go through life alone, I also didn't need anybody else to be happy. That I only needed to love myself and the rest would come.

I also recognized I would always be OK. That my deepest fears—of growing old alone, of being Jane Doe in a hospital bed with nobody to pluck the hair from my chin or bring me donuts from the outside—were just illusions born from a woman burning, grieving, and engaging in a healthy response to loss. Once the fog lifted, I could more clearly see that as long as I had myself, I'd never truly be alone. That the stories I told about myself and my worth in the past didn't have to be my future. And that I didn't have to follow convention or other people's expectations to have a happy life. That I deserved healthy love and all that it uniquely meant for me. That the only thing that kept me from loving another person and getting the love I deserved back was the fact that I had never really loved myself. Doing so finally gave me the safety I needed to let go time and again, both for what I wanted and with whom. And it will do the same for you too.

Chapter 2

THE STORY YOU
TELL YOURSELF

*I'm single and believe I lost my chance at love twenty
years ago. Long story. But I have to love myself, and I
have a lot of things to get over. I'm fat and ugly, and
before you tell me I'm not, just know I have a mirror
too. But I have to learn to love me and get past that. I
don't think I can, but I will try.*

—Callie, 53, Idaho

When I was twelve, my mother decided I needed to lose weight
and took me to Weight Watchers. I lost ten pounds. It was
a double-edged sword in that my mother, who'd lost twenty-five
pounds herself and was as devoted to the program as she was to
her marriage to my father, was happy. And I loved my mother
and I wanted to please her. But it was also incredibly frightening
because suddenly I had more to lose than just pounds.

If I gained any of it back—and there was a high probability I would, given I was not very disciplined at that age—I stood to lose my mother's love, approval, and acceptance. At least that was how it felt. Because while she was a good mom, who claimed to deny me food and put pressure on me to be thin *because* she loved me and wanted the best for me, she also made it clear she didn't always like me, especially when I was eating foods she hadn't preapproved as good for my waistline, or when I weighed more than she thought I should.

I remember those moments well. When she'd catch me with an unsanctioned pretzel from my dad's Charles Chips can or notice that my jeans were snug, she'd shake her head and proclaim in front of whoever was watching that I "didn't need that," pushing or pulling said contraband away. Once, for example, when I stayed home sick from school and some friends brought me a half gallon of rocky road ice cream, she scooped them each a bowl (none for me) and then shoved the rest frantically down the garbage disposal when they left. Then there was the time my aunt made her famous carrot cake for a holiday dinner and my mother offered it to everyone around the table but me.

This punishing and withholding behavior from an otherwise very loving mother was confusing for me, as I was only beginning to develop my relationship with food and my body. Back then, I didn't see the crime in having a tasty snack or putting on a few pounds. I certainly didn't think they warranted the anger, silent treatment, or retraction of love I perceived from my mother as a result.

And yet when they happened, she'd bury her head in her hands and wonder how she'd failed me. She'd stop buying foods she thought would tempt me or add to the "problem." The problem being *my* body.

She'd promise to take me shopping at my favorite stores if I would just control myself. Tell me how much happier I'd be if I ate only enough to keep my vital organs functioning. "You can never let down your guard or be happy with how you look," she'd say, using herself as a model, since she was always depriving herself of something to be thin.

On any given day, there was a lot riding on how much I weighed. So you can imagine how it felt to stand up in front of a room full of adults to receive my first pin for losing ten pounds at a Weight Watcher's meeting, my mother beaming in the front row.

It was a defining moment for us both. She was proud that I looked so good—how a girl looked was everything in her book. And I was proud that she was proud. That the problem of my body was no longer a burden to her, at least temporarily.

Looking back, however, I can also see how that experience— of standing up in front of the crowd, receiving all that praise for simply getting skinnier—also hurt me. How, despite my mother's best intentions, it ultimately put into that little girl's brain that she would never be thin enough, pretty enough, or good enough to have the love and acceptance that we all want. How I was much too young to be productively introspective about it all. Or understand how its message would burrow into my hippocampus like a tick and inform the choices I'd make in love and other areas as an adult.

Back then, things like choices and romantic love and adulthood weren't on my radar. Surviving was. Keeping my mother's love was. Which led me into a circular, three-step process for earning me her good favor: First, acquiring a taste for plain vegetables, bland chicken, and fish steam-baked in the dishwasher (a method she had read about in a magazine). Second, binge-eating fatty, sugary "bad" foods when she wasn't looking, like in the car, at school, or at a friend's house. And third, figuring out how to minimize the damages on the back end, literally and figuratively, so she wouldn't suspect anything.

It was tricky balance, and, frankly, I never mastered it. I was always in her doghouse, getting caught for eating what I shouldn't, failing to learn the crucial lesson that "nothing tastes as good as thin feels." A friend who had a similar mother did master it by becoming bulimic. Unfortunately for me, I was too much of a wimp to stick my finger down my throat to the point of actually vomiting. Instead, I just took my lumps . . . and then acquired this belief in the process: When you're thin, you deserve love. When you're not, you don't. And you should just take whatever you can get.

Unexamined Beliefs Define and Derail Our Efforts

According to Peter Halligan, a psychologist at Cardiff University, beliefs are "mental architectures of how we interpret the world," and serve as "our subconscious autopilot."[4]

This means that my subconscious autopilot—the mental architecture I took with me into the dating world—was to believe that I had to be a perfect size six to be loved. And if I wasn't, since my weight has always fluctuated, I should be grateful that I got any attention at all. Even if it was bad, cheating, lying, disrespectful, dirty-bastard attention.

When it came to love and relationships, I allowed this belief to take over my life because I didn't know I had a choice. I just accepted it, even though it was given to me when I was much too young to be complicit or really understand what I would get myself into by accepting it as the truth. (We'll talk more about this later.)

I, of course, attracted and was attracted to guys who, with the exception of Hector, cared more about how I looked on the outside than who I was on the inside. And I was a lot on the inside. I had big dreams, a big personality, and a big desire to not just receive love, but give the big love I held inside for fear of scaring the right people off.

The belief that I had to be a perfect size six to be loved made me appreciate any crumbs tossed in my direction by mostly awful guys, even if those crumbs (and the guys, for that matter) were old and rotten. Because when my mother got mad at me after discovering I'd eaten something bad for me—something I'd either smuggled in or that had fallen through her cracks—in the bathroom, with the fan on, while she slept, I knew she at least cared enough to feel something about it.

This is how beliefs work—by informing everything.

That includes the stories we tell ourselves about who we are and what we're worth. And those stories can take us in one of two directions. They can empower us at the point of decision-making (e.g., do we go out with that guy, accept that behavior, hold on or let go) to believe that we're worthy of the good things we want in life. Empowering beliefs are those that allow us to act resiliently, have faith in ourselves, and invoke positive thoughts and emotions.

Or they can disempower us. Limit the way we see the world and ourselves in it by reminding us in the most crucial moments that we're too fat, thin, tall, short, stupid, smart, easy, hard, aloof, needy, or whatever, to be worthy of the love we want. That we shouldn't hold out or wait for what's never coming. Instead, we should just settle before it's too late.

These limiting or negative beliefs prevent us from fulfilling our true potential. They're the ones that convince us, just as we're about to go out onto the stage, that we've forgotten to check for toilet paper on our shoe or that what we're about to say is just downright stupid. They hold us back, give rise to negative thoughts and emotions, and often sabotage our efforts at having anything good.

Whether limiting or empowering, beliefs sit just below the surface of our consciousness like a second skin, telling us what and how much we deserve and what we can reasonably expect from life and love. They drive the bus without our knowing it, while we're asleep in the back row, waking only when we arrive at our destination, often bewildered as to how we got there.

I knew this because I'd spent a lot of time at places I never wanted to go. With men who often had me asking, as I cried over them instead of vowing to choose better, what I'd done in a previous life to deserve them. I had let that belief that I wasn't worthy of love unless I was thin inform one bad relationship choice after another, until recurring heartbreak forced me to see that my failed relationships were less about the guys I'd selected and more about why I was selecting them. And what I believed about myself. After all, my life was the by-product of my choices, not theirs. (PS: So is yours.)

It became painfully clear that unless I took an honest and sometimes painful journey inside of myself to understand how my beliefs about myself and love were culminating in a reality I didn't want—and unless I held myself accountable in a *productive* and not punishing way (and you know how *that* talk track goes)—being in one unsatisfying relationship after the next would be my destiny.

What I learned in the process was that the only way to create change was to wake up to my limiting beliefs and redefine them as needed to serve me appropriately. Especially the one that had me believe I had to be thin to have happy, healthy love since the hard proof just wasn't there.

After all, I was thin when I met Tom. Leonardo da Vinci may have had the Mona Lisa. But I had Tom, my masterpiece of bad boyfriends. And he nearly crushed me.

Tom was the new sales guy at work, where I wrote for a small association publication in Chicago. Since he was shallow and valued appearance over all else, we were a perfect match. His attention both fed and validated me. And, in return, he got someone who not only adored him but also was willing to toss aside everything she was for whatever his ego, lies, and overall deplorable behavior had to offer.

Funny, because I disliked him immediately upon meeting, which I sadly discounted because I hadn't yet adopted the practice of listening to my instincts. In looking back, my lack of interest is probably one reason why he latched on so tightly, the thrill of the chase and all. This was despite the fact that he lived with a girlfriend, and I had a boyfriend named Lou.

I'd met Lou at a restaurant where we were both having dinner separately with friends and I couldn't stop looking at him, he was so handsome. In one of the boldest, most rom-com moves I'd ever taken, I wrote my phone number on the back of a napkin and asked the waitress to give it to him once we'd left. But unbeknownst to me, the story of how we met would be as interesting as he—and our relationship—would ever get. Because once we got into the nitty-gritty of actual dating, he had absolutely nothing to say or give. It was me who'd do all the talking. Who'd have all the insights of the day, news to share, or just plain silliness to impart, while he'd just sit wherever we were and look pretty. It helped that he had a fun-loving group of friends (which always surprised me) whom I really liked and who seemed to like me back. Fortunately, we spent a lot of time with them, which made the often-drowsy experience of being with Lou less so.

While Lou's personality was like anesthesia, Tom was a bad boy—loud, arrogant, obnoxious, selfish, and downright exciting. With Tom, at least I had someone with a pulse that beat more than the sound of water dripping from a slow faucet. Being with him was like binge-watching a well-reviewed, R-rated, much-buzzed-about series on Netflix. Sometimes so off-color you simply had to look away, but you always came back for fear of missing out. And yet the best part of Tom—the part that won me over to believing he was worthy of my romantic attention—was the simple fact that he liked me and how I looked, and told me so often. And this, I'm not proud to say, was the main criterion on which I based my decision to say "yes," back then, to almost anybody.

Tom was also very strategic about winning me over. First he became my friend, stopping by my cube to ask for help, telling me jokes and saying how pretty I was, getting me to open up about what I wanted from love, and then offering it up in a well-calculated drip campaign that, over a period of months, had me questioning whether my first impression of him had been wrong.

Eventually I ditched Lou and consented to being Tom's girl-on-the-side, at least until he ditched his girlfriend. Once he did, a few weeks later, he moved in with me and quickly proposed. My parents made us a brunch in Philadelphia so they could meet him, and he showed up five hours late, claiming he'd been in a car accident on his way down to Philly from New York City, where he was allegedly seeing "clients." My family disliked him immediately. But his excuses were good enough for me. My blinders were secure.

When we got back home to Chicago, I learned from a gossipy friend at work the real reason why Tom had been late to our brunch, and why he traveled so much in general. It wasn't because of a fender bender or even the requirements of his job, as I thought, but because he had a girl in every port.

I was devastated.

And while I should have been the one to toss him out of my apartment, it was his choice to move out and fast, while I begged him to stay (poor, sweet, sad girl). He moved back in with his ex-girlfriend—the one he'd left for me—and promptly began courting another girl at the office, rubbing it in my face until eventually we both left the company, and I never saw him again.

Not surprisingly, he went on to marry a Jazzercise instructor who was also one of the reps he'd worked with at trade shows and whom he'd claimed, on countless occasions while we were together, was "just a friend."

And I went on to lie on my sofa for months after, crying and snotty, binge-eating pizza and cookies, mad at him for being a liar and at myself for falling for such a con, until I finally had to acknowledge that something had to give. I was almost thirty. It was time to break the pattern and rethink things.

What did I believe about myself that had gotten me into such a painful predicament? After all, I was thin when I'd met Tom. Shouldn't that have meant something? Earned me the love and respect I deserved, like my mother gave me? Shouldn't he have been beaming at the sight of me? And if being thin didn't mean anything and he wasn't beaming, what did that say about everything I knew to be true—about myself, love, and relationships? How could I shift my own paradigm? Start making better choices? Understand what was happening?

Where did that work even begin? I would come over time to learn the answer, which was in exploring my own belief system, looking for cracks in my foundation that were tripping me up, and making changes as needed.

Because, again, our beliefs are powerful: in the best of ways when we choose them . . . and in the worst of ways when we don't. When we simply allow limiting beliefs to run amok inside of us instead of reining them in before they do us harm. Turning a blind eye can be dangerous because your beliefs may mislead you into thinking that you need to be, do, act, say, or think one thing in order to have healthy romantic love—when in reality, you don't. And yet you won't know that until you take the steps necessary to understand your beliefs and how they're informing your actions. Only then can you give them the proper perspective and flip them on their heads so they work for you instead of against you.

I had no idea that thinking I had to be the thinnest version of myself to be loved—the kind of skinny that was almost unnatural for my body, given my genetics, love of pizza, and slow metabolism—had me standing in my own way.

I thought it *was* the way.

It dictated and derailed everything. Had me doing things when I wasn't so thin that I look back at with shame. Like meekly asking for respect, knowing I'd stay even if I didn't get it. Saying I was sorry to keep the peace, even though I hadn't done anything wrong. Being willing to sacrifice all or part of myself to win or keep the affections of someone else. Accepting bad behavior because nobody is perfect, and who was I to ask for more, anyway?

Thinking that if I just waited around long enough, good men like Hector would give me everything I wanted.

Silly girl.

Which begs the question: How about you? What beliefs are standing in your way? Have you ever even stopped to ask the question? And if so, what's the answer?

Reaching the Tipping Point

Cindy, a thirty-eight-year-old nurse, was forced to ask and answer this question when she found herself in an untenable marriage, bumping up against some long-held beliefs that told her she had to stay in it . . . no matter what.

She'd been raised in a religious cult that had women defer to men in order to stay "in God's good favor." And so, at age twenty-one, she left the religion and, at twenty-four, met and married Martin.

"I loved how close Martin's big Italian family was," Cindy says. "They appeared to love each other unconditionally, and I'd never had that. There were always so many conditions to being loved and accepted in the cult. For the first time in my life, I thought I'd matter. I couldn't believe my good fortune."

But once in, Cindy learned not only that the family was highly dysfunctional but also that Martin lied, cheated, and verbally abused her. After they'd had their first child, Cindy convinced him to go with her back into the religion, since she still believed leaving him wasn't an option. After all, she'd learned, as a result of her upbringing, that on the hierarchy of needs, hers came last. She'd learned that she would never be strong or capable enough to take care of herself, that she needed a man for that job. And that she'd need to live by his and other people's rules in order to be loved at all.

Despite all of this, she thought going back into the religion would offer herself and her husband structure and community, and get them on track to being a happier family. Once there, however, despite her playing along, taking the three kids they'd eventually have together to Bible classes, and holding on to the belief that she couldn't leave her husband for any reason, nothing changed.

"Martin would still leave for days at a time, sleep with other women, take money out of our account, and blame me. I started to really struggle with the idea that I was bound to this guy, no matter what awful things he did," Cindy said.

She reached her breaking point when one day she found him holding their eight-year-old daughter, Candace, in the air by the back of her panties, laughing. When Cindy begged him to stop, he threw Candace on the ground.

"That's when I was done," she said.

She realized that even though leaving her husband defied her current belief system, it was time to take the risk and let go of that belief. Because while doing so would alienate her from the only religion, family of origin, and friends she'd ever known, it would also free her and her children from a horrible situation.

It was a risk she was ready and willing to take. And a decision that brought her to inconsolable tears.

"I had no other choice," she said. "I feared my daughter would hate me if I stayed and didn't give her a better life, one she deserved. I would hate myself for it too."

The morning after the incident, she left her husband and never looked back. "I didn't care anymore about being in God's or the cult's good favor. While it wasn't easy letting go of those old beliefs and all the people in my life that went with them, I felt relieved. I had no idea where our next meal was coming from, but those new beliefs—that I could take care of us without anybody else's help—carried me. They told me that something better was waiting and that we, that *I*, deserved it."

Cindy was one of the lucky ones in that she eventually realized the problem: she'd believed the wrong things about herself, things that weren't true about who she was or what she was capable of, or how she should or could go about her life. Things that kept her in a situation that was so bad, the only place she had left to turn was inward, to herself. The good news for her is that she was able to find her way out by, over time, turning limiting beliefs into empowering ones. The bad news is that too many others continue to avoid this exercise despite being desperately stuck, like she was, in the wrong relationships.

I suppose I shouldn't have been, but I was surprised by the number of women who wrote to me after my TEDx talk went live and who continue to write to me almost daily about their desire to let go and about how hard it is to get what they want from a partner despite their best efforts at being all they think their partners want them to be.

These women are so focused on what their partners are doing or not doing and why—holding true to beliefs that they don't even know they have and letting those beliefs determine their next moves—that they fail to examine the role they're playing in the situation or see that there's a way out. And it's well within their grasp.

This way out has them do the digging necessary to more productively understand their own motivations—and the belief systems that underlie everything they do and choose in their lives—and then change them (we'll talk more about how in the next chapter).

While these women may know intellectually—and even instinctively—that they need to go inside of themselves for answers and let go, they're not going there. They're paralyzed. Afraid to take the risks inherent in letting go of beliefs, and in turn partners, comfort, or familiarity as a result. Instead, they immerse themselves in the drama of the moment, dreaming up ways to fix whatever is wrong with their partner or situation. Anything rather than embrace the power they've had all along to look inward instead of outward and take charge of their own lives.

I know firsthand how much easier it is to ruminate on someone else's issues and deficiencies and excavate their motivations than it is to look unblinkingly at our own. After all, we may not be prepared for what we find or like any part of it.

I obsessed so hard and for so long, I was in a constant state of nausea. It's a wonder I ever found my way home.

Still, going inward is a far better option than walking around in circles day after day, dizzy inside of an unhappy situation. I also know, however, that a lot of people don't see it that way. Whether they're not ready, are scared to look too closely in the mirror, aren't sure how to create change or how they'll survive it, they'd rather spend time normalizing, coping, accepting, or deflecting their way through a bad relationship than putting their own belief systems under a microscope.

Unless and until, that is, they hit a tipping point and, out of ideas for getting to a better place, decide that it's finally time to look at the hardest parts of their relationships and deal with them. Even if it's painful.

Joy, a sixty-one-year-old writer, had a perfectly happy marriage with the man she'd married when she was twenty-one and he was nineteen—after, that is, they'd worked through a few issues in the early years of their being together. They'd both been brought up by large Midwestern, Catholic families and, as such, shared many beliefs, including one that stated divorce was taboo. That meant that no matter what challenges arose in their marriage, they'd need to either work them out or accept the situation.

Which was all well and good until they had their first child. That's when Frank announced he was going to night school to fulfill his dream of becoming a financial planner, leaving Joy to pick up the slack by working a full-time job, caring for their newborn daughter, and deferring her own dreams of being an author.

"Frank's decision to go back to school was not a decision we made together," she said. "And I resented it, especially since I was just starting to get attention for my work, which was not easy, because writing and publishing back then was mostly a man's game."

As several months passed and Joy examined her belief system, she decided that she simply couldn't remain silent. If she was working toward equal rights in the writing world, she could certainly have equal rights in her marriage, despite what her religious and conservative roots might have told her.

"I explained to Frank that if I couldn't get more time for my writing, I'd have to rethink our marriage," she said. This led them to counseling, where they examined the beliefs they held individually and made the necessary updates and compromises in order to stay together.

"We each had work to do in challenging the beliefs and even illusions we had about marriage that were ingrained in us from our families, that we hadn't yet had the maturity to process," says Joy. Together she and her husband broke through convention by developing their own rules for what constituted a happy marriage. They went on to enjoy a happy life together for thirty-three years and counting.

Like Joy, many of the women I spoke with acknowledged that in order to get to a place of being able to let go, they'd had to reconfigure deeply held beliefs to get closer to the healthy love and relationship they wanted.

This was the case for Chelsea, who, looking back at her failed twenty-year marriage and thinking about her dating future, said this: "I recognize that I need to rethink old beliefs I have about love and relationships. It's just going to take some time and work and, yes, bravery on my part. But I can do it."

Yes, she certainly can, and so can you. And it will all be worth it.

We Hold On Because We're Hardwired for Safety

So why is it that we hold on so tightly to our beliefs? Is it because we're defective? Weak? Lazy? Or simply too afraid of our own shadow?

None of the above. An enormous amount of research shows that we're hardwired from a very young age with a belief system that can either help or hinder us from finding the love we want.

Science supports this hypothesis. I could write an entire book about it, and many have. For our purposes, however, I'd like to home in on three key points:

First, we don't form beliefs as thoughtfully as we imagine we do. Yes, logic does not always factor in.

Second, what we believe is not necessarily true.

And third, and most fabulously, we can actually *choose* our beliefs. So, if we have a belief we don't like or find isn't serving us well, we don't have to accept it as being true. We have the option, the imperative, and the power to change it.

Now, let's unpack.

It will likely come as no surprise to you that we acquire most of our beliefs when we're children. Our parents have a lot of influence over who we are and how we see the world, as does the environment they create for us.

As I mentioned earlier, Bruce Lipton says that up until the age of six, we are holding on to everything we take in through our five senses. He and other researchers agree that we then subconsciously process this information into a belief system that serves us, depending on how we need to survive inside of our family dynamic. If it's a healthy one, we may form positive beliefs that teach us that "we've got this," and that we can do pretty much anything we set our minds to.

But if that dynamic is dysfunctional, we may invent a very different set of beliefs. The kind that are designed to help us avoid danger and create safety in that particular situation. The problem is that once we leave it, these beliefs will no longer work. To the contrary, if they're limiting (and there's a good chance they will be), they may harm us by keeping us in our own crosshairs, preventing us from getting where we want to go, and with whom.

Adding to the problem is the fact that, as human beings, we're physiologically programmed to do everything possible to validate and reinforce our beliefs. So if we're holding onto outdated, self-sabotaging beliefs from childhood, we may not reflexively stop to reevaluate or realign them when we're stuck. Or consider that what we have always believed to be true either no longer applies to our current situation or was never true in the first place. Can you imagine everything you ever thought of as real turning out not to be? They make entire categories of scary Lifetime movies out of these kinds of revelations. And while the plots always seem to work out in the end, getting there is very rarely pretty. It's no wonder we're so hard-pressed to buck the trends of our own subconscious.

Even once we're past childhood, we risk not being as thoughtful as we could or should be when it comes to developing self-serving beliefs. Because while we think we form beliefs logically and thoughtfully—by first hearing or experiencing something, and then deciding whether, in our infinite wisdom, we want to accept it as true or false—in reality, we simply hear something and immediately accept it as true, whether or not we've investigated it for ourselves.

In 1991, Harvard psychologist Daniel Gilbert summarized centuries of research on belief formation by saying that "People are credulous creatures who find it very easy to believe and very difficult to doubt. In fact, believing is so easy, and perhaps so inevitable, that it may be more like involuntary comprehension than it is like rational assessment."[5]

Two years later, he and two researchers from the psychology department at the University of Texas at Austin led a study that examined whether people could actually comprehend assertions without believing them. Through a series of experiments, they found that our default is to believe what we hear and read as true. In the study, subjects read a series of statements about a criminal defendant or a college student. These statements were color-coded to make it clear whether they were true or false. Subjects under time pressure or minor distraction made more errors in recalling whether the clearly marked statements were true or false. But the errors weren't random. Under any sort of pressure, the subjects presumed *all* statements were true and used them to make consequential decisions about the target, regardless of how they were labeled.[6]

In 1994, researchers in the psychology department at the University of Michigan asked study subjects to read messages about a warehouse fire. Some messages mentioned that the fire started near a closet containing paint cans and pressurized gas cylinders, encouraging them (predictably) to infer a connection. When, five messages later, subjects received a correction stating that the closet was empty, they still answered questions about the fire by blaming burning paint from toxic fumes and citing negligence for keeping flammable objects nearby.[7]

It turns out that truth-seeking—the desire to know the truth, regardless of whether it aligns with our beliefs—is actually opposed to the way our brains process information.

Here's another reason why we cling to our beliefs: evolution. Before there was language, the only way our ancestors could form new beliefs was by directly experiencing the physical world. For them, seeing really was believing, and there was little room for error. After all, miscalculating what you saw or heard rustling in the grass could very well get you eaten.

Back then, we didn't question our beliefs when they were about things we directly experienced, especially when our lives were at stake. But, as complex language progressed, we gained the ability to form beliefs about things we hadn't actually experienced firsthand—and tended to believe them just as strongly.

All of this points to the idea that we will do everything in our power to find evidence for our beliefs, even if they're not true and even if something is telling us otherwise, because we are set to think that doing so will keep us safe, and that changing or letting go of our beliefs is just too risky.

But in reality, holding onto old beliefs is often even riskier, especially when new information is telling us that our beliefs need an update.

Therein lies my point: if you're stuck in love, standing at the precipice of a hard choice, feeling your back against the wall, and have recently learned something new about your situation that changes everything (and you know it does because your gut is on fire), or if you just feel in your bones that something is off, it's time to stop and check yourself. Vet the beliefs in question. And then take clear corrective action.

The good news is you can totally do this without anybody else's cooperation or permission. You get to the drive the bus! Motivate yourself to keep your foot on the gas with the fact that your beliefs become your reality. Because that *is* the much-proven truth.

Take, for example, research in the field of creativity. Much of it culminates in the idea that if you *believe* you're creative, you will be. And if you don't, you won't. Is it that simple? According to research, yes. The first study to definitively show this took place in 1968, where researchers gave 1,600 four- and five-year-old children a creativity test in an effort to find innovators for engineering and design positions at NASA.[8] They tested these same children again when they were ages ten and fifteen and then compared those scores with a large sample of adults who also took the assessment. The results showed the following percentage of test-takers in each sample that scored at the "genius level" for creative imagination:

At age 5: 98%
At age 10: 30%
At age 15: 12%
As adults (average age 31): 2%

This study and others also showed that while you may not be exercising your creative genius at the moment, we all have the raw materials. And creativity can be regained and even cultivated through learning, practice, and risk-taking.

So why do so many people think they're not creative? Why, it's their limiting beliefs, of course. They may be comparing themselves to other people who are known for being creative, downplaying their own capabilities. They may be afraid of being judged, or believe they're more left-brained than right-brained and that you can't be both. They may also have been told they weren't creative when they were just kids.

There could be any number of reasons why a person acquired the belief that creativity wasn't their strong suit. In the end, it doesn't matter. What does matter is what they need to believe in order to be empowered in the moment: Do they need to know they have the imagination necessary to succeed and thrive in their current situation? Or do they need to feel stifled by inadequacy? I'll always choose the former. How about you?

This is just one example of how our beliefs control our reality—and how we can choose to create both.

Which begs the question: Why do some beliefs make it through to our conscious and subconscious minds, and others don't? It's all up to something called our reticular activating system, or RAS. And while that sounds very *Avengers*, it's really a thing and we each have one. Here's how it works.

Consider that we perceive the world with five senses that are on all the time. With no rest for the weary, you can imagine how much information we're taking in through them all day, every day. Sounds, smells, images, feelings, tastes, and actions, all coming at us 24–7. Add that each sense can have an incredible degree of complexity, and it will come as no surprise that we need a process for determining what makes it through to our conscious awareness and what doesn't. Otherwise, we risk imploding.

Enter your RAS.

A bundle of nerves that sits at the bottom of your brain, its job is to filter out any unnecessary *junk* so only the important stuff gets through. The RAS literally decides *for you* what goes into your conscious mind and what doesn't. It's the reason you learn a new word and then start hearing it everywhere, or why you can tune out a crowd full of people talking but snap to attention when your name is called.

Your RAS takes what you focus on and creates a filter for it, without you even noticing. It also seeks information that validates your beliefs, filtering the world through the parameters you give it. Your beliefs shape those parameters—so that you can interpret that information in a coherent and safe way. After all, having to reinterpret everything from scratch would be an awful waste of resources, so generalizations, labels, and approximations are all fair game.

We then shape each new experience to make sure it fits the jigsaw puzzle we've already created and have been working on for years, because it's most efficient. Why overhaul an entire system of belief for one single perceptual experience when you can just distort that experience to make it fit?

See where I'm going here?

And yet senses don't shape our reality, beliefs do. Since information gets filtered, chopped, and changed before it's processed, the filter—again, our beliefs—has more impact on our experience of the world than our perception does.[9]

Read that line again. Then one more time.

This is why if you think you're creative, you are. And if you think you're not, you won't be. Or if you think you deserve healthy love, you'll find it. And if you don't, you'll likely settle for less.

The RAS helps you see what you want to see and, in doing so, influences your actions.

With that said, there is a school of thought that suggests you can train your RAS, marrying your subconscious thoughts to your conscious thoughts by "setting your intention." That's where ideas like the Law of Attraction come in (this refers to the belief that you will attract into your life whatever you give your energy and attention to). Such ideas state that if you focus on your goals, your RAS will reveal the people, information, and opportunities that help you achieve them.

In *The Biology of Belief*, for example, author Bruce Lipton tells the story of a woman who took part in a clinical trial to test the efficacy of an antidepressant drug. The pills relieved her thirty-year experience with depression, and brain scans confirmed that the activity of the prefrontal cortex of her brain was greatly enhanced. Only at the end of the trial did she learn she'd been taking a placebo. Her belief about what the drug would do for her was responsible for her improvement.[10]

So what does all of this mean for you? That you don't have to be prey for unwanted beliefs. If you're not getting what you want, you have a duty, in the spirit of Big Wild Love, to investigate how your beliefs are running you off into a ditch. And then turn the wheel. Because, again, it's only when we understand the beliefs driving our actions and create new beliefs that better serve us that we can get out of our own way. But we have to be willing to go there.

In summary:

If you believe you won't ever find a suitable partner despite all of your best efforts, your actions will reflect your belief. You will filter out opportunities around you, find evidence to rationalize your belief, and/or do whatever it takes to protect it.

If you believe you don't deserve healthy love, your actions will reflect your belief.

If you believe you're destined to be alone, your actions will reflect your belief.

If you believe your several failed attempts at love will dictate future attempts, your actions will reflect your belief.

If you believe you're too old to find love again, your actions will reflect your belief.

If you believe a happy union requires you to defer your own wants and needs to someone else's, your actions will reflect your belief.

If you believe it's OK to settle for less because you'll never find what you really want, your actions will reflect your belief.

If you believe you're a victim in your own love story, your actions will reflect your belief.

If you believe that everybody else deserves love except you, your actions will reflect your belief.

If you believe that your partner's needs, wants, and feelings are more important than your own, your actions will reflect your belief.

If you believe that you're not pretty enough, thin enough, or good enough to have the love you want, your actions will reflect your belief.

I've got all day, people. But I think you get my drift.

Change your limiting beliefs, change everything.

Knowing My Beliefs Were My Playbook, I Changed Them

That's where I started. Embracing the idea that my beliefs had become my playbook for action, and that if I really wanted to find healthy, lasting love, what "had to give" was my current playbook. I had to burn it like bacon.

I had to get right in the face of the belief that I had to be a certain size to be loved and run it out of town, show it who was boss'. I had to crawl my way out of the rabbit hole of believing that I was a victim and wondering why these relationship failures *always happened to me.* I had to reckon with the idea that nothing was "happening" to me. That I was inviting it in. All of it. The bad boys. The unacceptable behavior that I more-than-willingly accepted. The one failed and disheartening experience after the next.

None of it was random. It was all the product of my faulty beliefs—like an old, broken transmission that simply refused to turn over. These were the same beliefs that had once protected me in childhood, earning me the love of a critical mother, and I was duly grateful for them. But I wasn't grateful for the way they were completely derailing me as an adult looking for healthy, romantic love.

It was only when I faced the truth of what I believed about myself and, specifically, my body, that I was able to turn that belief on its head and, in response, make choices that would ultimately get me where I am today. Most days, doing a Snoopy-like "happy dance" of gratitude.

Did it happen overnight?

No way. I had plenty of work to do. In fact, it's work I continue to do every single day. The good and bad news is that I was inspired to stick with it by (a) a lengthy string of disappointing experiences that could have easily driven me to the bottle in a very bad way and (b) the fact that I was nowhere close to where I wanted to be in life and love.

And you can too.

As I turned over the stones of my limiting and empowering beliefs (yes, I had both, and you probably do too), I learned to do three really important things:

First, I stopped blaming other people, including my mother and inanimate concepts like *fate,* for where I was, because neither one had anything to do with it. I'd been an adult making my own choices for a very long time.

Second, I took responsibility for my choices and my mistakes, without beating myself up or trash-talking the person I was for making them. To the contrary, I was hell-bent on learning something from them and proud of myself for finally taking my lessons.

And then, lastly, I figured out how to make new and different choices—ones that would ultimately restore my faith in the idea of love and bring me closer to having the kind I wanted with both myself and someone else. With a willingness to change my beliefs, I also changed the lens through which I saw potential partners and myself.

By investigating who I was through the belief system that drove me, I was able to make peace with the idea that beliefs are just illusions we cling to as a matter of fact. But they're only real if we say so. And nobody is holding us to account but ourselves. We have the power to change our beliefs anytime we want.

As I peeled back the layers of what I'd been taught to believe about myself and, in turn, my worth, I came to see that I needed to rewrite the script. And that I actually could—that creating a new version of my beliefs and, in turn, my experiences was infinitely possible.

In the end, the dating near-death experience that was Tom served as not only a shining reason to curse and eat enormous amounts of potato salad, but also as one of my life's greatest gifts. It forced me to face the truth of what I believed most profoundly about myself . . . to my detriment. I'd let my beliefs call the shots for far too long. While it was painful to survey the damage, it was also a relief to know that it wasn't too late to do something about it.

It was only once I did that I went on to meet Hector. Sweet Hector. This internal examination moved me further up the ladder toward what I knew I wanted. But it was definitely a process.

The good news was I was finally in it, and my choices were getting better, since Hector was one of the good guys. The bad news was I wasn't all the way there yet. But I would be. New beliefs would set me straight.

Chapter 3

NEW BELIEFS IN PRACTICE

I suffer from borderline personality disorder as a result of my childhood trauma. My father and stepmom were awful to my brothers and me, and as a result, I am utterly terrified that my boyfriend is going to leave me. Every night I sob over whether tonight is the night. Then I saw your talk, and it hit me how much I needed to let go of the past and believe that I'm worthy of him staying. I'm not the little girl at the mercy of her abusive parents anymore. I know I need to keep working on these issues, but your words help. Thank you!

—Sasha, 26, Sweden

I remember the day well. For some, it was just another hot and sunny Tuesday in August. For me, it was one of the biggest days of my life: moving day.

I'd already told Hector we were done. Sold my condo, quit my job, squirreled away enough Chicago pizza in my belly to hold me for several winters, packed my whole life into boxes, bought a townhouse four states away, and hired movers to get me there.

And now a moving truck the size of a small diner was tightly parked on my narrow city block, holding up traffic and pissing off the neighbors.

Today I would say my final goodbye to the life I'd had in Chicago for almost two decades. Leaving the city for New Hope, Pennsylvania, land of artists, farms, and wineries, would be a radical change, like going from the Barnum & Bailey circus to Gilligan's Island. But I was ready for it. Eager to slow down and figure out what—and who—was out there for me and who this new *me* even was. I'd hoped that a change in landscape would give me the perspective I needed to see what came next, along with a chance at a fresh start.

And I needed one. I longed for a chance to live in the beginning of something, since I'd been living in an ending for months. Saying goodbye to Hector, my office, my apartment, my friends, my colorist, my dog walker, my favorite sushi restaurant and pizza joint and coffee shop, and even the "me" I'd been previously—the one who came to Chicago in her twenties and would leave as a woman on the brink of menopause. As I looked back at the time in between, I couldn't help but wince at the horrible choices I'd made in dating. They'd paved the not-so-yellow brick road that led to this moment.

All of this *ending* felt like a corpse on my back. Spending an extended period of time knowing I'd never see or be with someone or something in quite the same way again was crushing. I had the heating pad and empty cupcake wrappers to prove it.

The good news is the body is resilient if we take our lessons, which I was hell-bent on doing. Particularly when it came to the flawed thinking that had gotten me stuck in the first place.

I was ready to turn the page on the outdated beliefs given to me when I was a child in the sixties, when Tang, the banana seat, and console televisions with only three available channels were our greatest novelties. It was time to put the obsolete thoughts I had about myself and love back there with them. Hold them under an imaginary microscope and brain-hack my way into a more progressive alchemy.

I would be my own chemistry experiment, using newfound courage to say goodbye not only to the romantic road to nowhere but also to the beliefs that kept me on it. That included those that said settling for less was my destiny.

That how much I weighed had anything to do with the way I loved another person or myself.

That I'd aged out of love and my best years were behind me.

That leaving the twelve-year investment I'd made in another person was like throwing all the money in my 401(k) into Lake Michigan.

That I was a failure, a spinster-in-training, a pox on my family because I hadn't followed convention and gotten married.

That there was only one way to have a happy life and it required the love and acceptance of another person, preferably someone tall and rich and Jewish.

I was ready to say goodbye to these and any of the other limiting beliefs that had kept me safe as a child needing to placate a critical mother, but failed me miserably as an adult looking for a healthy love relationship. In that scenario, relying on my beliefs was like treating cancer with Advil.

Sitting on the curb outside my soon-to-be-former condo, listening to the neighbors cursing, and watching my possessions line up in the moving truck like soldiers at gunpoint, I contemplated the internal process I'd need to undergo to rewire a lifetime of thinking. The good news was I was up for the challenge. The bad news was that I'd have to be if I wanted any of this upending to mean something. You've heard the saying, "Wherever you go, there you are." Yeah. That's what I was afraid of.

It was all so pat. I knew what I had to do, and I was doing it. Yay for me. And then, the heart palpitations came. Wait a minute, that's my sofa going into that truck. My bed. My computer. My first-night box.

That was my stuff. *All* my stuff.

What if I changed my mind? Could I rewind this movie? Get it all back?

For a split second, while the movers struggled to get the oversized sofa on which Hector and I had watched movies—slept, cried, had hard conversations, the sofa we had embraced as if it were another person in our relationship—through the narrow door of my building, it dawned on me: there really was no turning back.

I hugged myself, pressing my arms against my body. Of course I'd had these moments of doubt and fear before, but that was when moving was just a concept. An obscure goal that lived only in my mind, that I could work to vigorously achieve as if I were training for an Ironman. That would happen someday, but certainly not now.

But it was happening.

Oh my god, it was happening.

I inhaled. And then again. And then again. I pulled myself in a little tighter and closed my eyes. And when I opened them, it was still happening. I was still there, in the chaos of change. I was doing this: I was leaving . . . something I'd thought about doing for years but hadn't been able to bring myself to do for real. The very idea of it had been like a noose around my neck, choking me so hard I'd thought I would never survive it. For the longest time, I hadn't dared to actually do it . . . uproot myself and say goodbye to the life I'd built in Chicago.

Say goodbye to Hector once and for all.

And yet, here I was: still in one piece, solid matter, with a heart beating like Ringo Starr playing the drums in his prime. I was not only surviving this movie, I was directing it, calling the shots, sitting in the big chair.

And suddenly, it felt *good*. Winning-the-lottery good. First-kiss good. Deep-dish-pizza good. Trip-to-Paris good. Little-black-dress good. Best-massage-ever good.

First-I-love-you good. Because, in a way, it was my first "I love you"—to me. Leaving Chicago was one of the very first gifts I gave to myself, in the spirit of Big Wild Love, that moved the dial of my life for the better.

Turns out I was stronger and more resilient than I'd ever realized or given myself credit for. The key now would be to keep going. To not let fear, regret, doubt, or any of the hundreds of songs that would remind me of Hector and my life here any time I heard them (I'm talking to you, Marc Anthony) take me down.

I could do it. I had to.

Exercising Our Power

More recently, I received a letter that, unfortunately, didn't end with its writer letting go. It came from a twenty-eight-year-old woman in the Philippines named "Rhoda," asking for advice. In it, Rhoda explained that she had spent a year with a guy who made no apologies for being emotionally abusive to her. Among other things, he put her down, was overfriendly with other women, insensitive to her feelings, and controlling in terms of when she could see her friends and family and pursue her graduate studies. Despite his bad behavior and her doing everything she could to make him happy, it was never enough. And while she knew the relationship wasn't leading to the marriage she wanted, she allowed herself to get lost in it anyway.

By the time she'd finally mustered up the courage to leave her boyfriend after a year, she'd dropped out of her PhD program, severed her relationship with her family, and suffered from anxiety and depression.

Three months into their separation, as she worked to rebuild her life, she remained heartbroken and unsure of how to let go entirely, without risking going back to him. That's when she wrote to me.

In her note, she said that, while she would have liked to "believe" she was a strong, independent woman who could move forward without her partner and be happy, she was struggling.

Wow. Talk about the answer being right under your nose. In her own words, she wanted to "believe . . ."

I pointed this out to her. That the answer for moving forward was right in front of her, as it was for so many other women I'd spoken to over the course of my research. But as I said, Rhoda's story didn't end with her replying a month or two later that she had finally let go. In fact, I never heard from her again. As far as I know, she's still struggling, or she could even have gotten back together with her boyfriend, although I certainly hope not. I hope she came to realize, by examining and reframing her limiting beliefs, that she could do better for herself.

In chapter 1, we explored how the pain that comes up in this work is like going through a tunnel. Like Rhoda, all the women I'd spoken to had the power to work through that pain by going inward. But they didn't know how. They didn't want to see that it could be as simple (but certainly not easy) as understanding and reconfiguring their beliefs. Or they were so lacking in Big Wild Love they didn't even want to try.

What Rhoda's story shows us is how incredibly difficult it can be to shed the beliefs that aren't serving us. I wanted so badly to help her see that if she turned all that sad, fearful, desperate energy inward, she'd be able to dig her way out. That in examining her beliefs, not only would the pain eventually abate, but she'd be setting herself up for success the next time out of the gate.

In fact, exploring our beliefs when life isn't giving us what we want is one of our most underused superpowers. Which begs the question: Why aren't we going there?

For one, we're afraid of change, and looking inward may result in our having to do it. "Ninety percent of the reason why I'm employed is people's fear of change, even if it's for the better," says Dr. Suzana Flores, psychologist and author of *Untamed: The Psychology of Marvel's Wolverine.*

Second, we're physiologically hardwired to accept our beliefs without question, especially if we think we're in peril, as we so often do when we're staring down the barrel of heartbreak. It's an evolutionary survival technique that still has us using the mechanisms of fight, flight, and freeze, instead of examine, to get by. So, if you feel threatened by a problem or situation, your natural instinct will be to try to fight or outrun it, take flight by pretending it doesn't exist, or freeze and do nothing while it festers.

Your natural reflex won't be to stop, breathe, and contemplate which of your childhood beliefs is keeping you stuck in a relationship situation that could very well land you on the *Real Housewives* series. Oh, if only it were that easy.

But that's just not how our biology—or Hollywood—works.

While I can't tell you about the ins and outs of reality television, I can tell you that stopping to examine our beliefs can and should be reflexive. Even if our physiology doesn't help, our awareness, participation, and a healthy dose of Big Wild Love can pick up the slack and make all the difference. Unfortunately, we're often woefully low on all of those things. While statistics to support our collective self-worth are scarce, in 2005, the National Science Foundation did publish an article that showed the average person having twelve to sixty thousand thoughts a day. Of them, 80 percent are negative and 95 percent are exactly the same repetitive thoughts as the day before.[11] Proof that we're both really down on ourselves and really stuck.

Even if we are strong enough to change our beliefs, actually using the new-and-improved versions is another story. Because while we mean well in vowing to abide by them, once their novelty wears off along with the pain that triggered them, we often find ourselves back on autopilot, reverting to old ways of doing and thinking.

A Shift in Thinking

So what's the answer? While we know from the previous section how hard it is to do this work, it's certainly far from impossible. On the contrary, by being hyperconscious of the fact that your beliefs dictate your actions, you can shift what those beliefs actually are. But because beliefs are such intangible things, it's actually helpful to look at that concept in reverse: that different actions can actually lead to different beliefs. This means that a good place to start embracing something as intangible as a belief is by taking tangible actions that are well within your *conscious* power. Like, for example, examining your beliefs, which should go arm in arm with cultivating Big Wild Love. In fact, this should be the first course of action when you find yourself stuck or unsure how to move ahead. Whether that's deciding if you should go out with someone, stay with someone, get back into the dating game, take a break, prove fate wrong (you are *not* destined be alone, OK?), or lift the vow of celibacy.

Only you know when it's time to shake things up and initiate the process of change and letting go. What I'm saying is that when the time comes, you can take action by checking your limiting beliefs at the door.

That's precisely what Jess, a forty-three-year-old program director and advocate for women in business, did when faced with unexpected tragedy in her relationship.

She and her husband Stuart had a tumultuous marriage. The beliefs given to her during a difficult childhood had her working overtime to keep him happy and her stuck in a five-year relationship that had been troubled from the start.

"Growing up in the Bronx, we were dirt poor, and my mother used to feed us mayonnaise sandwiches; of course she doesn't remember that now," Jess told me, adding that she'd been estranged from her family for years. "My mother didn't know how to be a mom. When I was sixteen, she told me that I'd be the kind of girl she'd have been jealous of. She hated how independent I was. And she brainwashed my three brothers to believe that I was mostly selfish, even though I tried to provide for her when I got older and she shot me down, preferring to live in a depressed neighborhood."

As a result of the belief given to her that she was self-centered, Jess did everything she could to make her husband, Stuart, happy—except give him the child he so desperately wanted. She already had a daughter from a previous marriage, and she'd had her tubes tied prior to meeting Stuart. While he pressed her to reverse the operation, she wound up needing a hysterectomy for medical reasons.

He never got over it.

So Jess became the *perfect* wife. Everything Stuart wanted, she did: had his food ready and his slippers waiting when he came home. Whatever he didn't like, she changed. "I did everything I could possibly do to give him a reason not to feel upset or let down."

Their life together got so bad that they vowed to reevaluate their relationship after Jess gave an important presentation she'd been working hard on. But that reassessment never happened. Instead, Jess got the call that Stuart had been killed in a motorcycle accident. "We'd said that, no matter what happened, by the New Year we'd be living our best lives, and then this happened."

After Stuart died, Jess started questioning everything she knew to be true about him and love. "I felt badly about not giving him what he wanted and could have blamed myself for being insensitive and selfish, but I was determined not to let the Pandora's Box of beliefs I'd gotten from my dysfunctional parents impact how I moved in this situation, because I knew that I was a very good wife," she said.

She also found out that he'd lied about their finances, saddling her with debt she didn't know they had, and had cheated on her with his ex-wife and several other women he was talking with on social media.

"Of course I was devastated, but our relationship was always complicated," she said. "I also knew the issues were his and not mine. And that, in the wake of his death, if I didn't work through my own pain and issues, I'd be in trouble. I just didn't realize how much I had to do that until he was gone and I was forced to see who he really was and how much I'd sacrificed for him." Motivated by grief and the need to heal and refocus, Jess took a vacation. Not being one to either rest on her laurels or play the victim, she sat under a palm tree and spent a productive four days grieving, processing, and figuring out a plan for moving forward. "Sure, I was a mess. I'd just lost my husband. But I was also tough and determined to make sure that everything would be better at the end of all I'd have to go through to process Stuart's death. Things had been so rocky between us, I couldn't allow him to control my happiness in his absence. I also couldn't let the beliefs I'd gotten when I was young manifest in my becoming a triple hot mess. I needed to be responsible and accountable to myself."

The good news was Jess knew herself well. As a result, she understood what it would take to go inward and get where she needed to go. She spent the time staring at the ocean, listening to music that moved her, and writing in the journal she'd long used to work out problems in her life. She relied on her faith and spirituality to get her through the toughest moments, allowing strong beliefs and her church to play a pivotal role. She cried, a lot. Had one conversation after another with Stuart in her mind, so she could both scold and forgive him for his indiscretions.

She talked to God.

She left those four days ready to take on whatever came next. And while she knew it would take a while longer to recover from her loss, she had the confidence of knowing that she'd be OK. After all, she had herself.

Then January came. And while Jess didn't look for it or expect it, or even believe love would ever happen for her again, she met Robert through her church. Having recently lost a cheating spouse himself, he not only understood firsthand what Jess was going through but also would become her best friend and confidante, offering her the kind of relationship she couldn't have imagined for herself just a year earlier. After two years together, during which they both worked through their respective grief, she'd come to align her beliefs with the idea that she deserved someone as honorable as Robert. And they got married.

Before her husband's death, Jess believed that she had to sacrifice large parts of herself to be loved. But as a result of Stuart's death and moving through the process of letting go, she realized that as long as she loved and stayed true to herself, she'd find her way to the right person when she was ready. Someone who would not only value her but also celebrate and honor her strength, independence, and resilience.

"It's funny, but in the New Year, I thought Stuart and I would be deciding whether to stay together or get divorced," she says. "I had no idea I'd meet someone else. You never know what's coming down the road. Change is not easy, but it's unavoidable. When it happens, you've just got to face your fears without letting anything you don't want in your head get you down. You've just got to keep walking."

Better Beliefs in Practice: A One-Day Detox

So now that you know the hold your beliefs can have on you and what you attract into your life, let's talk about how to create them in a way that sets you up for massive success. There are three key steps you can take to make sure your beliefs align with what you want from love—and what you don't.

In the spirit of the forty-eight-hour detox outlined in chapter 1, I'm going to recommend that you do a one-day detox (of course, you could always take more time if you'd like), either at home or somewhere outside of it—wherever you'll feel most relaxed and least distracted by everyday tasks and responsibilities. If you remain at home, be sure to unplug everything and put away your devices. It would otherwise be very easy to numb yourself to the very things you're looking to investigate.

All you'll need is a "belief journal," which could be as simple as a spiral-bound notebook from the drugstore, and a willingness to go deep and get real with yourself. Remember, like the previous detox, whatever you write will be for your eyes only, so feel free to "go there."

8:00 a.m. Do three pages of longhand, stream-of-consciousness writing about what you want most from love in your life at this very moment. What would make you happiest? Where are you falling short in having these things? How can you fill in the gaps?

8:45 a.m. Have a healthy breakfast, or whatever is your morning ritual, and prepare for the day.

9:30 a.m. Meditate or go for a gentle walk, do yoga, stretch, or perform some other light form of exercise—whatever clears your mind and gives you energy.

10:00 a.m. Step One: Identify your current beliefs

You'd be amazed at how many people don't know what their beliefs are. And yet your core beliefs, hidden beneath your conscious brain, are everything when it comes to what you think, feel, and do in life. You can't cultivate a benevolent set of beliefs if you don't know where you're starting from. Here are a few exercises to work through in your journal to help you figure that out. They're designed to get you deep into your current beliefs.

If, as you work through them, you find that you're writing the same things over and over, fantastic. That's confirmation that you're getting the clarity you need to move forward. Just keep your hand moving, and everything you need to know will be revealed!

Exercise #1: Complete the following sentences.

Write down as many answers as you can think of. Look for what you say to yourself when things go wrong and/or look the bleakest.

Relationships are . . .

Love is . . .

I am . . .

I choose . . .

People are . . .

Success is . . .

Life is . . .

Dating is . . .

Marriage is . . .

Most men are . . .

Most women are . . .

Exercise #2: Complete the following sentences.

- I had no idea that I believed _____ about myself.
- I had no idea that I believed _____ about my relationship.
- I believe that I deserve _____ from my partner and I don't deserve _____ from my partner.

11:15 a.m. Take a break. Make yourself a cup of coffee, go for a walk, or just sit and breathe deeply as a way to let your ideas sink in.

11:45 a.m. Go back to completing the following exercises:

Exercise #3: Review your notes for limiting beliefs and highlight them.

How do you know if a belief is limiting? It will not only feel bad in your body, like a bra that's two sizes too small, but present as negative, and it is likely to involve the following topics: safety (it's not safe to love), willingness (I'm not willing to open up for love), deserving (I don't deserve love), readiness (I'm not ready for love), ability (I'm not able to love), and wanting (I don't want to love, which can usually be tracked back to a bad experience).

You can also identify limiting beliefs by:

- Connecting them to the results you're having in your life. If you don't have what you want from love and relationships, you can probably track it back to a limiting belief.

- Seeing how the thought of a partner, idea, goal, or dream feels in your body. If, for example, the idea of going out with a certain person has you wishing you were going for a root canal instead, you may want to cancel.

- Looking for beliefs that keep you from being happy and peaceful, like "I'm always going to be alone" or "Something is wrong with me" or "Nobody will ever love me."

- Reversing the process. Thinking about what's not working and tracking backward.

Exercise #4: List three of the limiting beliefs you uncovered that you feel are most relevant to your current life and goals. Then respond to the following questions.

Where did you get these beliefs?

Are they true? If so, how do you know? Where's the proof?

How are they manifesting in your life and love?

Do they keep you safe?

Are they getting you what you want?

If not, what are they not getting you that you want?

1:00 p.m. Meditate, skim a magazine with light content, take a nap, rest. Do anything that doesn't require too much thought. This hour is designed to let your subconscious absorb and process this morning's work.

2:00 p.m. Step Two: Create new beliefs

This is the time to replace your limiting beliefs with more empowering versions that are better aligned with your goals. Before you get started, you'll need to acknowledge three important things in order to be successful: first, that you play the most powerful role in what you believe, even if you don't know how; second, that your beliefs do indeed create your reality; and, lastly, that you have everything you need within you already to create beliefs that will get you what you want.

Got it?

Great. Now, answer the following questions in your belief journal:

- What do you want from life and love? Try to answer as best you can, even if it's at a high level; we'll go deeper in the next section.
- What belief(s) would get you where you want to go?
- What's more important to you: safety or having what you want in life?
- Do you want to change your belief(s)? Do you think doing so will make a difference? Who else do you know with this belief, and do you feel aligned with them? Would you like to feel aligned in this way?

- What beliefs do the people you emulate have? How do those beliefs feel for you?

Based on your answers and what you learned from the morning exercises, look at each of your three limiting beliefs and decide how you'd ideally *like* to think, feel, and act around them going forward. Based on your answers, you'll write down a new *empowering* belief statement for each. Here's how that looks.

Let's say your current limiting belief is this: I'm too old to find love again.

Ask yourself how you'd like to think, feel, and act differently around that belief. Would you like to believe that you're the perfect age to find love, whether you're twenty or seventy? That all of your experience and knowledge acquired as a result of your life have led you to this moment, where you have much to offer another person? That there are lots of options out there for you? Are you feeling intrigued by the possibilities? Inspired to become the best version of yourself so that you can attract a healthy partner? One who mirrors your Big Wild Love and stands to benefit from all you have to offer?

Do you see where I'm going here? This is starkly different from "There's no way I can compete against younger women. I'm too old. Too wrinkly. Too fat. Too jaded. Too set in my ways. I've seen the dark side of love and, believe me, it won't change. I feel sick to my stomach just thinking about the disappointment of going back out there, only to be rejected time and again. I'd be a fool to even attempt it."

If you were a healthy prospect for love, which person would you like to have coffee with?

Instead of focusing on the negative thoughts, feelings, and actions that instruct your subconscious mind to search for more of the same, revise the anchoring belief.

So, instead of this: "I'm too old to find love again."

Write it as this: "I am happy and in the prime of my life and have so much to offer the right person. I can't wait to meet him/her when the time is right."

Now that's someone I'd like to have a large, skim, no-foam, two shots of sugar-free vanilla latte with!

With all of that in mind, make a list of your current beliefs. Play around with them and have fun. This is the good stuff—you deciding what you want to create for the future. Then, for each limiting belief, make a list of two to three new, empowering beliefs, because it's always good to have options.

Here are some more prompts to help jog your thinking in terms of how to do what I'm suggesting, especially if you are struggling. Using the same example of I'm too old to find love again, ask yourself:

- How would you advise a friend to reframe this belief? You may be getting stuck because you're too close to your own thoughts, biases, and feelings to come up with an alternative belief. If that's the case, approaching the question from a different perspective—how you'd counsel a friend—may get you the distance and objectivity you need. You might tell your "friend" that they're not too old to find love again. That, in fact, they've never been better or had so much to offer another person. Poof! There's your empowering belief: "I've never been better or had so much to offer another person." Now, hold that up against what you want in your life and love and see if it works. If it does, great. If it doesn't, keep problem-solving. Use the prompts that follow to help.

- How would a trusted friend, family member, or coach advise you to reframe the limiting belief?

- What don't you want? Take the opposite point of view.
- What would you like to get from the belief as a result? Work backward from there.

Again, there are no right or wrong answers here, just what works for you. While I'd like you to be thorough in your contemplation, don't take so long that you wind up with analysis paralysis. Spend about thirty minutes tops rethinking each new belief.

4:00 p.m. Treat yourself to something special: a pizza, a glass of wine, another nap, an hour in the garden, an episode of *Dr. Phil*. Whatever makes you happy. You've earned it.

5:00 p.m. Make dinner. Take the time to whip up some real food instead of grabbing something from the convenience store. Enjoy the ritual of preparing a meal. Let your mind wander and rest.

6:30 p.m. Write down each new belief on a small piece of paper and post them in visible places in your home: the bathroom mirror, just above the trash can. Once you have made a new list of beliefs, ask yourself if believing each one will make a positive difference in your life. If not, go back to writing. If so, it's time to make them stick. There are a lot of ways to do that so they eventually become reflexive. Let's go there next.

7:00 p.m. to 9:00 p.m. Relax. Watch TV, take a hot bath or shower. Prepare for bed.

Let all the hard work you did today sink in with a good night's sleep. That will set you up to begin using your new beliefs with awareness the very next morning.

The next twenty-eight days. Step Three: Make beliefs stick

Do at least one or more of the following every day, and then write about it in your belief journal either before you go to sleep at night or when you first wake up in the morning.

- Think about your new beliefs all the time. When you're on the train, making dinner, sitting in traffic, etc. Set them to music that makes you feel good to create a positive association. Before I wrote my TEDx talk, I played my theme song ("I Really Want It" by A Great Big World) every morning on the way to work, while imagining myself in front of an audience, to help me believe I could get there. And look how that turned out! Ask your subconscious mind to help you manifest new beliefs in reality.

- Tell yourself a new story about your life that features your new beliefs. For example, if you felt like you were invisible in a previous relationship and old story, replace it with one that has you as a vibrant part of another person's life. Bring in the new core belief that you deserve someone to put you first. Who are the main characters in your new story? How do they act and feel? What are the results?

- Visualize new beliefs in action as if they're already bringing you what you want, since science shows your brain can't tell the difference between what you're imagining and what's really happening. Engage your RAS by thinking about a goal or situation you want to influence and the result you want. Then make a mental movie about it and play it often.

- Look for evidence that reinforces your new beliefs. That means watching with awareness how the process of changing what you believe creates results in your life, because it's difficult to keep doing something *consciously* that doesn't serve you.

- Surround yourself with people who have similar beliefs, especially if they're getting the results you want. Find them and copy them.
- Develop a stronger belief in yourself. While you're working on cultivating better thoughts, work on cultivating a deeper level of self-love too (you can't have too much, trust me). List and affirm all of the wonderful things that make you uniquely you. Like, for example, your sparkling personality. The way your lipstick never comes off, even when you eat. Or how you parallel park like a champ. Even if you don't think it's amazing, write it in your journal and give yourself a little credit, would you?

Once the twenty-eight days are over, keep going! Use your new beliefs with confidence, since that's the whole point. Call upon them to guide your choices in love. Remind yourself that old beliefs no longer exist because they weren't doing the job. Keep your belief journal close so you can check yourself for old-belief creep, and write down any thoughts or ideas you have while experimenting with new beliefs, since you may need to try them on for a while. It's OK if, after a reasonable period of time, you decide you need to modify them because you're not getting results. There are no rules here. That's the beauty: you can believe whatever you want, whenever you want!

And if a limiting belief is too deeply ingrained in you to recreate, stay aware of it and reframe it in the moment as needed in conversation, relationships, or decision-making.

As you use your new beliefs, don't judge yourself or internalize other people's judgment if a belief doesn't serve as you'd hoped or you find yourself slipping backward. Just course correct. And recognize that judgements are simply projections that don't have to derail your progress.

Lastly, be patient with yourself. Recreating new beliefs takes time. And if you find an old belief trying to wheedle its way back in, remind yourself who's the boss here.

You are.

Driving from Chicago to New Hope I had with me a carful of boxes, my dog, Sophie, and, I'll admit it, a set of beliefs that were only just beginning to tug at me. As I started to overhaul my external life, I was doing the same internally. On that drive, I realized that to truly change the picture of who I was and what I had, I'd need to take a closer look at the filters my mind used to make decisions, beliefs being highest on the list.

And so I did, and quickly. Once settled into my new place, I started taking inventory of my most current beliefs, asking myself in the mirror how each one was or wasn't getting me where I wanted to go. If a belief didn't serve, I tossed it into an imaginary garbage can. And if I wasn't sure, I looked for ways to revise and reframe until the belief made sense for what I wanted in this next phase of my life. Healthy love. Happiness. Fulfillment.

It was an exciting and important exercise that allowed me to create a carefully curated set of beliefs to use in defining how my new life took shape. I was committed to doing it right.

In the end, I wound up swapping out the limiting beliefs around aging out of love and everything else I stated at the outset of the chapter for these more empowering versions:

That I was in the prime of my life, and my best years for finding love were ahead of me.

That I was grateful for the lessons I'd learned over all of the time I'd spent dating because they were necessary for the growth that would ultimately lead me to the right person.

That I was embracing my best life on my own terms, and it felt really good to be me.

That there were a lot of ways to enjoy a happy life, and they all started with loving and accepting myself. Anything that came after that was a bonus.

And that was just the beginning. I reframed so many outdated and expired beliefs, I felt almost ten pounds lighter after letting the worst of them go. Not only did creating new beliefs set me up to attract the right people and situations, but coupled with Big Wild Love, it allowed me to shift my perspective to create the change I'd so desperately needed. And it can do the same for you.

You just have to be open to doing the work, which is sometimes hard, but always worth it. I can tell you firsthand: without revising my beliefs and coming to love myself most and always, I'd never be where I am today. Which is someplace wonderful.

Keep reading.

Part Two:

THE
SIX-STEP
PROCESS

Chapter 4

THE EPIPHANY

*Recently I had a major disappointment in a relationship
that led me to a surprising epiphany. As a result, I let go of
my partner, realizing that, despite our being together for
years, he just didn't have my best interests at heart. And
now, just two short months later, my life is completely
different. That epiphany really changed everything.*

—Maritza, 38, Germany

Over the course of Hector's and my twelve years together, I
had many epiphanies—short bursts of clarity that revealed
the bigger truth about our relationship. These epiphanies would
present clearly to the unbiased and uninvested, like friends and
family, that he would never give me the long-term love and commitment I'd started to crave after our sixth anniversary.

But to me—the desperately biased and invested—they were
like stars shooting south. Which is why I did what any pain-avoidant
woman would have done in the same situation: I ignored them.

I ignored the fact that he'd grown less available to me over the years. That his excuses for not visiting my family with me—or doing anything that required real planning, for that matter—had grown longer and more frequent. That he'd stopped spending the night (in year eight) so he could "get home" to care for his aging parents, who lived upstairs from him in a duplex apartment.

With each epiphany, instead of waking up, I went back to sleep. While I rested, each unattended tremor formed cracks in our relationship's foundation that deepened and widened over time, until the ground beneath me rattled and shook and almost swallowed me whole the day I lay on that stranger's bathroom floor.

There were several epiphanies I'd had that could have spared me that experience, if I'd paid attention. But I didn't.

A therapist named Jody handed me one of these epiphanies, or rather clubbed me with it.

In year eleven, I'd somehow managed to convince Hector that, after some unproductive discussions about where we were headed, we should see a counselor to talk about it. A friend of mine, who knew our story well, recommended her therapist, Jody. Said she was "no bullshit." Perfect, I thought. A straight shooter. Just what we needed to help us move forward.

I couldn't wait to sway Jody to my side and get Hector the help he needed accessing his true feelings. Because, after armchair-diagnosing him, I was sure he wanted to be with me forever. He was just scared of abandoning his family, getting too close, having what he didn't think he deserved, or being truly happy. (Isn't this what we say when the men we love don't give us the love we want in return?)

First we each went to see Jody by ourselves, then together. The goal during my individual session was to make her see how advocating for my side was in the best interests of both. Then Jody would have my back.

After all, I'd found her. She owed me.

Once Hector and I had both had our sessions, it was time to all sit down together. I was excited to finally get answers, imagining they'd be in my favor. Hector would have his own epiphany, realizing he needed to put a ring on it. There'd be pound cake and coffee at the end. Tears. Hugs. A promise to invite Jody to the wedding. Minnie Riperton's "Lovin' You" playing us out of the building.

But then . . .

We barely had our coats off when Jody looked at me and said this: "Leave him. Now. You're talking about marriage. He's talking about house repairs and his mother's birthday. Never speak to him again."

Wait, what?

What about pound cake? What about Minnie Riperton? What about, *"You two are a swell couple who should be together forever—don't let this one get away, Hector!"*

While he looked dumbfounded, I felt like I'd been whacked in the back with a crowbar. It took everything in my power not to drop to the ground. We stood there, jaws open, as she asked him to leave the room—for good. And when he did, after some protest, she got so close to my face I could see her mustache. "Don't even let him drive you home tonight. Cut off all communication entirely, unless and until he gives you what you want. I don't think he will, but then you'll know for sure."

By the time I left, I felt like I'd been waterboarded by my own tears. I didn't want to believe any of it, even though I knew in my gut . . . she was right.

Of course, Hector was waiting for me outside, making promises he just couldn't keep. I quickly buried the gift of that epiphany.

While Jody's take-no-prisoners approach shocked me, it simply wasn't enough to scare me straight. I still wasn't ready to hear the truth. But I would be. Deep in my subconscious, where thoughts and ideas go to gestate and process, I was working it out. Jody's words, on a loop, were preparing me for epiphany number three. The one that would finally revive me from the dead and give me the fortitude to do what was long overdue.

To let go.

Sleepwalking through Epiphany

People have epiphanies all the time. These intuitive experiences, flashes of insight, strategic intuitions, sudden bursts of revelation, visions like that of a kaleidoscope changing—whatever you want to call them—are often gifts in disguise. The manifestation of our subconscious mind, an epiphany allows us to see the answers to our most vexing problems without realizing that we were even thinking about them. They have the power to wake us up to the truth of our situations so we can actually do something about them.

And I can tell you: once you have an epiphany like the one I had in that stranger's bathroom, there's no turning back.

Which is precisely why so many people brush them under the carpet. Because while epiphanies offer a unique opportunity to save oneself, these "aha" moments only work if people are willing to acknowledge the message. And all too often, they're not.

Instead, they do what I did: sleepwalk their way through. Sit idly by while their ship slowly sinks in a storm, despite the rescue boat just yards away, throwing out rope.

They don't grab that rope because they're just not ready for what happens if they do. They don't trust that the boat is real or that they'll survive what comes next; they're not willing to admit the painful fact of what that boat is trying to tell them.

Like Janice, a forty-three-year-old novelist, who lives in a quaint river town with her now-fiancé. When she married her first husband at age twenty, she thought marriage and family would be enough for her, but she realized very quickly that they weren't. That Collin, the high school sweetheart she'd married, may have been perfectly "nice" but didn't ultimately share her priorities.

While she loved Collin, she also married him at a young age because she'd grown up in a violent household and he offered her safety. She *believed,* based on what she was holding on to from childhood, that being with someone safe was all she needed in relationship to be whole.

And yet by the time the last of their three children had been born, she'd come to realize that safety wasn't enough. Desperately unhappy, working six part-time jobs while raising a family, she imagined enrolling in graduate school to pursue her dream of being a writer.

That's when she had her first epiphany, in the form of a benign brain tumor. It was a scare that reminded her life was short and inspired her to begin plotting her escape from the marriage.

It just took longer than she anticipated.

As her children got older and she and Collin became more financially stable, Janice was finally able to enroll in school. There, she gained the attention of literary agents. She also met and fell in love with her now-fiancé, but she vowed not to act on their attraction until she could leave her marriage.

That's when epiphany number two struck.

"One night, I found myself bawling in the living room while everybody else slept," she says. "I didn't see any way to succeed at what I wanted to do as long as I stayed with Collin. We were just too different. It was like someone else was in the room with me, telling me to slit my wrists. It scared the shit out of me."

The next morning, she told Colin she wanted a divorce. "Once we told the kids, I was able to finally see my life. Now I wonder why I waited twenty years to do it. It's funny, the epiphany that threatened my life ultimately saved it. I just wish I'd listened to that first one."

And she's not alone. For many people, it can often take several epiphanies to sit up and finally take notice. Those who do often feel regret for not having woken up sooner—while others never get there. Instead, they ignore those subliminal taps on the shoulder indefinitely, enduring days, months, years, and even decades of potentially unnecessary anguish.

"In looking back, I know when my first epiphany happened, but sadly, I didn't do anything about it," says Christine, a fifty-two-year-old nurse who's been divorced for ten years and, now single, lives on her own. She recounts the story of how, toward the end of her marriage, her daughter Julia was getting ready to go to a party when she called her husband to ask for his opinion about something she wasn't sure of. He was traveling for business, which he did often.

"All I needed from him was a gut check, but instead he overreacted and told me Julia couldn't go at all," she says. "Easy for him to say, at the airport, while I was the one at home dealing. Of course, we had a fight. That's the moment I realized he didn't have my back."

Christine says she fell apart after that. While in hindsight she can see that epiphany for what it was, back then the incident left her weak and confused, struggling to see it as a sign that things were starting to turn and that her husband didn't love her anymore.

"He was changing the rules, after we'd agreed I would make decisions for the kids while he was gone," she says. "But still, I didn't let go. Instead, I ignored that epiphany and focused on coping for more years than I care to count, until I was ready and willing to take a bold step out the door. I'm just grateful that I was able to get there. I know not everybody does."

When Epiphany Strikes, Listen

The takeaway from these and so many other stories is this: look alive, people. When epiphany strikes, sit up and pay attention. Don't let it go by or wait for another to come around the bend. Because there are no guarantees it will. Instead, be willing to embrace the message—painful and scary as it may be—and be ready to take action on whatever it's telling you, especially if it's telling you to let go. Because that message is the buried treasure. The pot of gold at the end of the rainbow. It's the truth that will set you free, but only if you let it.

And you must. Because let's stop kidding ourselves: you know the truth of that epiphany. You do. In fact, you must know it in order for that epiphany to happen. After all, you can't bake meatloaf without meat. You look away because you wish the truth were different.

I get you. I didn't want to accept that Hector would never commit to me, either. I wanted a different truth. The Disney-fairy-tale truth. I spent years throwing tantrums in my head over the fact that my truth would not end like this: Hector in a white linen shirt and perfectly pressed blue jeans, me in a bohemian white dress, with long hair and chandelier earrings, surrounded by our friends and family wishing us, the newly married couple, a lifetime of happiness.

To compensate, I made the problem about my being defective. It must have been me . . . misreading him and the situation, being impatient. Unlovable. Undeserving. If I'd just checked myself or learned to be happy with less, it would've gotten better. Maybe morphed into a younger version of myself, wide-eyed and dewy-skinned, weighing in at a perfect 128 pounds, wearing a year-round uniform of thongs, tank tops, and tight Levi's. (Don't men like that?) It would've all been OK.

I went into a virtually breathless state dancing around what I actually *knew for sure* for the better part of a decade. Swiveling and shimmying and shaking my way around it so fast and furious, all because I simply didn't want that truth to be what it was.

You know the truth of your situation as well. You just don't like it any more than I did. Well, that epiphany is your chance—to step up and do something. To act boldly on your own behalf. From asking for what you want in relationship and speaking up, to ending things, starting again, moving on, getting back out there, going within, pushing past your fears, giving the finger to limiting beliefs, cultivating kinder, gentler, and more productive ones in their place, and most importantly, radically loving yourself like it's the best and only job on the planet.

Trust that epiphany has come to you in response to your own subconscious SOS. That it's showing up for a reason. If you do, it will be scary and hard and challenge everything you thought you knew about yourself and your situation. Just take a very deep breath and go with it.

Let an epiphany shake you in your boots, and then walk tall through it. Because it's only once you do that you can begin the journey toward letting go of what's not working and finding what will.

That's also why epiphany immediately follows the cultivation of Big Wild Love. Because your ability to take action is defined by the clarity you have in forming it. Working with that epiphany will get you there.

Just ask Elise Ballard, actress and author of *Epiphany: True Stories of Sudden Insight to Inspire, Encourage, and Transform.* She was struggling in her own unhappy marriage when she was suddenly "sideswiped" by the truth of why she just couldn't let go.[12]

She was working in a show, playing a woman who loves her husband but can't have a baby. Then her character finds out that he's had a one-night stand and gotten that woman pregnant. They break up, but by the end of the play, she and her husband get back together and they adopt his baby with the "other woman." During her weeks of rehearsal and research for the role, Elise told the prop master that she would find the adoption agency brochure for her character to hand to the other woman onstage. While printing the brochure for opening night, she was struck by an epiphany.

"It came to me that a major reason I stayed in my marriage was because, being in my thirties, I feared that if I left, I might never have a biological child of my own. It was so real and deep and terrifying that, until that flash of insight, I hadn't been able to admit it to myself. And it had been paralyzing me from leaving.

"The epiphany freed me because I realized through my research for my acting role how many ways there are now to become a mother, and if that's what I wanted, being terrified of not having a child of my own (with someone I was miserable with anyway!) was no reason for me to stay in a marriage that was never going to work no matter what I did.

"I was so in denial. I could have never let go if that epiphany hadn't hit me, and more importantly, if I hadn't listened and believed in it and finally taken some real action."

This is how epiphanies work. Elise got a divorce. And then wrote a book about it. In it, she recounts other people's stories of how they used epiphanies as wake-up calls to both their purpose and to course correct.

Every single person I interviewed whose epiphany positively changed their life took the first step toward whatever the epiphany compelled them to do, even if they had no idea what would happen after that.

And if you're lucky enough to have an epiphany, so, too, should you.

Like Alex, a thirty-six-year-old writer and photographer who lives alone in the city. She was dating a new guy she really liked when her doctor changed her prescription for birth control and she had a "hormone-induced meltdown" in front of him. "I was mortified," she said. "When I apologized, he very politely accepted. And then I never heard from him again."

After a short period of heartbreak, self-doubt, and kicking herself for "ruining everything," she had an epiphany. "I was washing my face one night and suddenly thought, why was I so concerned about what he thought of me? After all, his behavior was terrible. He apparently didn't know how to communicate or accept an apology."

It was an epiphany that lingered just below the surface until she was ready to take its lessons. That's when she started asking new questions. Like did she really want him?

Then there's Lissa, an accountant who, at thirty years old and single, is searching for both the right partner and the reason why she can't find him. "After dating too many men who were just wrong for me, I long for a sign to guide me," she says. "What do we do if we are looking for that light and it's just not coming?"

Good question.

Making Lightning Strike

Based on my research and general observations, people have epiphanies because they're ready for them. They have the information they need to formulate answers to their most pressing quandaries. Some people, like Lissa, may even be praying for an epiphany to guide them, contemplating what it would be like to experience this fierce moment of revelation, while others are in absolute crisis mode and desperate for a sign telling them what to do.

Wherever folks are in the process, what they share is a readiness and receptivity to an epiphany. They've set their intention toward change, even if they're not quite ready to act on it. And they trust the messenger, which is often the voice of truth coming from inside themselves, which they can no longer squelch.

Which begs the question: Is it possible to conjure up an epiphany if you want one? And if so, how? Truth be told, most of the information that addresses these questions is purely anecdotal. Science knows very little about that brief moment when we just *get it.*

There was one study, however, done at The Ohio State University and published in 2017 in the *Proceedings of the National Academy of Sciences*, that sought to identify the factors that contribute to having an epiphany.[13]

Scientists Wei James Chen and Ian Krajbich used eye-tracking and pupil dilation technology to see what happened as people figured out how to win a strategy game on a computer. They could see study participants figure out the solution through their eye movements as they considered their options, and they were able to predict who was about to have an epiphany before they even knew it was coming.

For the study, fifty-nine students played a game on a computer against an unseen opponent. On the screen were eleven numbers (0 through 10) arranged in a circle. The study participants chose one number and then their opponents chose a number. While the details of how the game was won are complex (it had to be so the participants could have something to figure out), the optimal game strategy boiled down to picking the lower number. Picking zero was always the best choice.

The participants played thirty times in a row, always against a new opponent, while an eye-tracker sitting under the computer screen could tell what numbers they were looking at as they considered their options. After each trial, participants could either commit to playing one number for the rest of the trials, or vary. They were then reminded what number they'd chosen, what number their opponent had chosen, and whether they had won or lost.

The results showed that about 42 percent had an epiphany at some point and committed to playing zero. Another 37 percent committed to another number, suggesting they didn't learn the right lesson. The remaining 20 percent never committed to a number.

Participants gave clues along the way that they were about to have that aha moment—that zero was the best choice—even if they didn't consciously realize it. The eye-tracker showed they looked at zero and other low numbers more than others just before their epiphany, even if they ended up choosing other numbers.

Chen and Krajbich also found that those who had epiphanies:

- Spent less time looking at their opponents' number choices and more time considering the result of each trial, whether they won or lost.
- Learned suddenly. They weren't building up confidence over time or paying a lot of attention to the "commit" button until the moment they decided to hit it.

- Experienced significant pupil dilation while viewing the feedback screen (telling them whether they'd won or lost) before they made the "commit" decision. Dilation went away after they did.
- Showed signs of learning before they made a commitment to zero.

What were the key takeaways of this study? That you have to look within to truly experience epiphany learning. And that it's better to think about a problem than to simply follow others.

While not definitive, the results take into account that epiphany comes from having a deep focus on your choices and how you've come to them.

This, along with the stories of epiphany I've gathered from my own research, leads me to believe that we do have some power in inviting epiphany into our lives. Here are a few ways to do it:

Believe epiphanies can happen. As you know from earlier chapters, beliefs play a powerful role in creating our reality. It follows that setting the stage for epiphany requires you to believe that it actually exists. That you can be struck by lightning in a way that's productive in offering solutions that have eluded you in the past.

Not sure if you're a believer? Here's a way to find out. Ask and journal around the following questions: Do you believe epiphanies are possible? Why or why not? If you don't, what will it take for you to believe they exist? Just keep your hand moving. If you do, you'll learn a lot about where you stand.

Create the right conditions for epiphany. That means getting quiet and into a listening state. Science tells us that when we do, we're more likely to turn our attention inward to make insightful connections. And when we're distracted from the day-to-day pressures and routines, our subconscious is freer to work a problem more creatively.

To get here, ask yourself: Where do you get your best ideas and/ or feel most relaxed? What time of day is it? What are you doing? Then consider trying the following approaches:

a) Go back to the Two-Day Relationship Detox outlined in chapter 1. Apply some of its principles to your day-to-day life.

b) Walk in nature.

c) Talk to a friend.

d) Contemplate your navel (yep, just sit there and do nothing!).

e) Gaze at the sky and allow yourself to daydream.

f) Listen to music.

g) Write.

h) Meditate.

i) Take a bath or shower. I don't know about you, but I get a ton of ideas and thoughts in the bathtub! So much so that I keep a notepad and pen nearby. Interestingly, research shows that our brains give us our best ideas when we release a lot of dopamine, and taking a warm bath or shower does the trick.

The key is doing whatever puts you in a calm, safe, and contemplative space, so you can be present for whatever comes in. There are no right or wrong answers here. It's finding what works uniquely for you—from tending your garden, for example, to participating in a support group out with people you trust.

This is precisely what was done by Kim, a forty-eight-year-old florist who is single and lives alone. After enduring an abusive marriage for twenty-four years, she was desperate for help. After being molested by a babysitter at the age of eight and never telling anybody, she married her high school sweetheart—"a wonderful guy with a heart of gold"—at age twenty-two. She didn't know at the time that he was also a closet alcoholic. And over the course of their marriage, he grew increasingly out of control and abusive. "He made me think I was crazy," she says. "There were a lot of secrets in our house, and a lot of shame."

Desperate for help and concerned about the impact of their volatile relationship on their three daughters, Kim finally went to Al-Anon. "I just sat and listened at first until things started to shift inside me," she says. "After a few months and a lot of love from the group, it struck me that I was dealing with a thirteen-year-old boy in an adult body. And that I couldn't fix or change him. I'd been so afraid to leave. He'd convinced me all the problems in our marriage were my fault and that if I left nobody else would ever love me again.

"Those meetings gave me the strength to see the truth but push past my fear and shame to let him go and believe I'd be OK. They taught me the value of loving myself."

Do something new. That means getting out of your day-to-day environment, meeting new people, and having new experiences.

Like Jackie, an artist who, at forty-five, was in a five-year relationship with a guy she loved but who couldn't give her the commitment she wanted. After living in New York City for so many years, she'd always dreamed of buying a house upstate. She imagined she'd buy it with her boyfriend, Ray, until one day she decided to do it by herself.

"I never planned on buying a house alone, but I came to the realization that I'd have to shake things up with Ray in order to get anywhere," she says. "I also always wanted to be a homeowner, and just doing it, well, that felt like the smart woman's choice."

Little did she know at the time, doing something new would change everything. Within three months of moving, she'd ditched Ray. And shortly thereafter, she met the man she'd live and own a business with. "No one was more surprised than me when John moved in," she says. "I had no idea that creating so much movement would have such an impact. I also didn't know how it would all turn out when I made the decision to listen to that epiphany, but I couldn't be happier."

Be on the lookout for epiphany. Especially when you're in need of reflection or trying to make sense of a situation. Write down the question you want answered before you go to sleep, and wake up and journal around the answer. Here are some questions to consider: When was the last time you had an epiphany? What did you do about it? What did you learn from it? Where are you currently struggling in love? If you were to have an epiphany today, what would it tell you?

Just be careful of "duds in disguise," says Elise. "Great ideas in the middle of the night can seem so perfect, but in the clear light of day they're just not something you want to do." Instead, let it simmer for a few days and sink it. You may find it's the seed for a better idea or just plain bad, in which case you'll be glad you held off on pursuing it.

Allow yourself to live in a state of uncertainty. Many years ago, I wrote a column for *Shape* magazine, and I worked with a therapist who told me, "Too many people who are in limbo—uncertain in light of a breakup or just after—feel the need to rush to fill the void, but I don't recommend this." Instead, it's best to let yourself experience your feelings and live in a space where you don't have all the answers, keeping in mind that discomfort has its purpose. It's designed to help us recognize when it's time to make a shift or ditch something that's not serving us.

Welcoming discomfort and contemplation without expectation is the best way to invite epiphany in. Because that's when your subconscious is at its freest. Every woman I talked with told me they had no idea where their epiphany might take them. But they embraced the gray space and remained open anyway. And that made all the difference.

"I had my epiphany on a yoga mat," says V. "I had feared so many things in life. My epiphany told me to dive headfirst into that feeling, and to the things that scared me most, so I'd know I could survive them once and for all. The only way to grow and let go was to be OK with not knowing where I was going. I let the love I had for myself guide me."

From Epiphany to Action

I can personally attest to the fact that epiphanies can change your life. Three was the charm for me, and I'm just grateful that I was able to see the gift—of that meltdown in somebody else's house on the North Side of Chicago—for what it was. A desperate cry for help coming from within. A flash of light so all-consuming, there was nothing else for me to do but try to climb my way inside it.

In that moment, I wasn't sure I could survive a realization that hit me like a truck falling from the clouds. But I did. I used that epiphany to traverse a new course on new ground. I had no idea where it would lead me (back to myself, folks) or that it would compel me to let go so big and hard that my entire world would shift on its axis. But it did. And I am so grateful.

I now believe that it's the universe's divine wisdom to make what happens next, after epiphany, a mystery. Because if we knew, it might make us even more gun-shy. In hindsight, knowing how deeply and broadly my life would be upended might have been a deterrent to accepting that epiphany's message. But being on a need-to-know basis gave me what I needed to put one foot in front of the other: instructions. Permission to take one bite, one chunk, one baby step at a time.

Let go of this man, it said. *It's OK. You're OK. Start here.*

I learned how to navigate life post-epiphany as it happened, along the way. And it all worked out fine . . . even better. But I wouldn't have any of the good stuff I have today if I hadn't acknowledged and then acted on the crashing cymbal that alerted me to one of the most monumental moments of my life.

That epiphany rebooted my operating system. It had me born again in the best of ways. And it can do the same for you.

Let it in.

Chapter 5

THE AFTERMATH

When my boyfriend of twenty years started to have doubts, I decided it was time to let go. It's been hard, but now I'm starting to see the new me, and I like her so much more. Now I'm free to dream—what kind of husband will I have? He will be over the moon about getting me as his wife. Most of all, I don't need to be afraid anymore. I can be myself and not some lamer version who tries to fit into a role that wasn't meant for me. I feel so grateful. I have absolutely no bitterness or anger left.
—Ellen, 35, Finland

Over the course of our relationship, Hector and I took two breaks in the hope that space would not only offer us clarity about where we were headed, but put us on the same page. Hector initiated the first break after we'd been together for eight years because I was pushing hard for marriage; it lasted one week. He caved quickly, promising to talk more seriously about our future and even getting a place together. When those things never materialized after several months, I initiated another break.

I never for one second had any intention of making this break permanent. I just figured that, in lieu of an ultimatum (which I knew Hector wouldn't receive well), I'd give him time to reach his own conclusions about life without me. I was sure he'd hate it and capitulate to taking the next step.

But it backfired. The person who really suffered during that break, which lasted several months, was me. I missed him. He was my best friend and champion, and not being able to see or talk to him left a gaping hole the size of Jupiter in my universe.

It also left me to fend for myself in taking care of my beloved golden retriever, Sophie, while I traveled for business, which I did a lot back then, because before the separation Hector would always stay at my place and watch her. I needed a Plan B. Trouble was, I didn't have one.

Fortunately, I had generous friends who offered to take Sophie in as long as I brought her to them in the suburbs, which was fine since they lived in a nice big house with a big yard. I figured Sophie would love that. And sure enough, I was right, given how she raced into both when I dropped her off. The good news was it was comforting to know she'd be OK while I was away. The bad news was that, after three days, she didn't want to leave. And when I came to get her, she ran in the opposite direction.

My God, I was crushed.

My friends, of course, felt awful, rambling on about how it must be all the green grass, grilled steak, and chew toys they'd given her and not that she wasn't happy to see me. But all I could think was, *Never mind the snub, how will I ever compete with a yard?* One with a sprawling garden and lounge chairs with big fluffy pillows and several feet of green, littered with tennis balls. My city deck, which overlooked an alley, was the size of a small dryer. The only thing it was littered with was actual litter blown up by the wind. It also didn't help that my friends both worked from home, which meant that Sophie always had company.

I couldn't remember a time when I'd felt so unwanted and inadequate, and that was saying a lot since I was already woefully low on Big Wild Love. And now not only was I failing in my relationship, but even the dog didn't want to be with me.

After finally coaxing Sophie into the car and getting on the road to home, I tried to console myself using logic. "It's OK, Jill," I said, holding back tears. "Sophie loves you. She's just missing Hector too." But not even a mile into the thirty-mile drive, I lost it.

Those tears came as fast and as furious as the cars whirring by me at breakneck speed. I pulled quickly onto the shoulder and let it rip. A tow truck pulled up beside me, but I waved him off. How pathetic I must have looked sitting there curled over the steering wheel, my shoulders rocking, howling and hyperventilating, my furry child in the back seat refusing to even look at me. To make matters worse, I noticed we were seriously low on gas.

Shit. Shit. Shit. Shit. Shit.

All this emotion—it couldn't just be about Sophie not wanting to leave her version of paradise. It was Hector. All the feelings I'd bottled up and disassociated myself from as a coping strategy were bubbling up and out of me like a sump pump in a rainstorm.

I couldn't get my arms around where we were. How did we get here? What happened? What had happened since those early days when we couldn't bear to be apart? When all we wanted to do was be together, and he was loving and present and *there*. I'd had so much hope for us back then.

And now, well, I felt lost. Tired. (So tired.) Unlovable. Ashamed for having stayed as long as I did.

I felt old and so alone. That's when I realized how familiar a feeling it was. That apparently, it was my relationship *normal.* I'd gotten used to it.

Which begged the question: Did I really want to be with someone—anyone—who made me feel alone all the time? If I cared at all about myself, the answer had to be no. After all, what would I have told my girlfriends if they'd come to me with the same question? (Ditch him!) And yet there I was. I'd invested years in this feeling. Whether this break had offered Hector clarity or not, I couldn't ignore the clarity it was offering to me . . . in Technicolor.

It was a heart-palpitating moment, like finding yourself about to crash head-on into the car in front of you when your brakes suddenly stop working.

It was obvious: I needed to let go. Unless Hector surprised me at the door with a proposal or some tangible promise of it— which I knew, based on past history, was about as likely as my waking up on Mars—we were for all intents and purposes done.

I sat there for ten minutes that felt more like a million, my adrenal glands pumping out cortisol like gasoline. I couldn't do it, wasn't ready. It was too big, too overwhelming, too much to think about, since letting go wasn't just about Jill and Hector anymore, but rather about who Jill was. It was a question I was not prepared to answer, because while I'd thought about what it might be like to leave him, I'd never stopped to contemplate who I'd be on my own. It had been so long since I was.

And yet here I was, rocking in my car, another epiphany, after the one I'd had during our session with Jody, hitting me like a meteor. And I ignored this one too. Kept it buried for two more years until it raised its ugly gift of a head on that stranger's bathroom floor and I was finally ready for it—and let go once and for all.

But I have to wonder: If I'd allowed myself to process my feelings after that epiphany and keep trucking—if I'd asked myself the hard questions instead of distracting myself with things that didn't matter, like work and travel and gas, distancing myself from that epiphany's consequences—could I have saved myself twenty-four months of agony and confusion and let go even sooner?

Who knows, right? (And yes, the answer is yes.)

To Feel, or Not to Feel

How about you? You've had an epiphany about your relationship, life, or inner self that's telling you that you need to let go in some way. Maybe you need to let go of a whole relationship, someone you've been dating who just doesn't feel right, a belief that's leading you astray, an emotion that feels bad in your gut, or a behavior pattern you know is sabotaging your efforts at love. Whatever it is, that epiphany is showing you the light. It's telling you what you need to do. The question is: Will you listen?

(Say yes.)

And if you do listen, how do you even know where to start?

Let's say you've just let go of a relationship and you're raring to date. After all, that epiphany sure was freeing. Let's also say your ex made you roaring mad. And while you're done with him, you remain pissed. Still, you're not giving him one more precious moment of your life, so you just "let it go" or "get over it" without feeling that rage for one more second or taking the time to understand where it comes from (likely you being mad at yourself as well) and what you need to learn from it. After all, you're done with that loser.

Then you meet a great guy. He has a job, his shirts are ironed, and he can drive at night. You race into a relationship—anger still simmering under your nail beds like a bad fungus. You then project said anger unwittingly onto this great new guy who doesn't deserve it by flying off the handle when he asks how your day went or flinching when he tells you he's into beekeeping. If he's big wild loving, he won't stick around to pay for the sins of another, so he's out of there. And if he's not big wild loving, well, good luck with that. Two non-big wild loving people do not bode well for having a healthy relationship. This is reason enough to deal with the anger before you get out there and in front of a great guy. That way, when you do, you won't project anything but your best, most lovable, and gloriously imperfect self.

I could write an entire book of examples like this, but I'll give you just one more to drive my point home. Let's say you didn't take the time to feel your feelings or check in with your beliefs as a result of an epiphany, leaving yourself prey to all kinds of destructive thoughts (and, as you now know, bad thoughts lead to bad things).

Turns out, a new limiting belief has crept its way in to your psyche as a result of your negative experience, or an old limiting belief you thought you were long past has been revived from the dead—take your pick. But you don't know that, because your subconscious is like the mean girl from high school: it's hiding things in a way that's not helpful, is trying to take you down, and has very little meat on its bones.

This is precisely what happened to Dawn, a thirty-six-year-old physical therapist, after she left her cheating husband, Craig. One of the reasons she married Craig was because he came from the big, happy family she never had as an only child but always longed for. Once married, however, she'd had the quick epiphany that his meddling and judgmental family wasn't all that happy. And by the time she left it, she'd transformed the once empowering belief of "Big, loving families are wonderful, and I'd like to be part of one" into a limiting belief that said, "Big, loving families are bad, and I need to stay away."

After taking very little time to process her feelings, and even less time to examine what happened that led to her split from Craig, she moved quickly into her next relationship, with Trent. Trent didn't speak to his family. And Dawn was more than OK with that. In fact, based on her new limiting belief, it was a selling point. "He thought it might be a problem," she says, "but I assured him it was actually a good thing."

While Trent didn't interact with his family, he did struggle with drug addiction, hiding it from Dawn until after they were married. Although she'd had her suspicions, she'd never let it give her pause. She figured if she didn't acknowledge it, she wouldn't have to deal with it.

Then, Trent relapsed . . . three times. It took Dawn three tumultuous years to accept that the marriage was over, because she didn't want to grapple with the feelings of shame and failure that came with being twice divorced in her thirties. She also didn't want to look in the mirror and acknowledge that it was a mistake she could have prevented if she'd only taken the time and energy to better understand who she was, where she'd come from, and what she'd be getting herself into.

If only she'd taken the time to face her feelings. All of them.

This is just one of the things that can happen when you don't do the inner, emotional work necessary to move forward positively and productively after an epiphany. As Dawn's experience and so many others show, bottling up your feelings, ignoring red flags, or holding onto a grudge, anger, hostility, limiting belief, and the desire for revenge doesn't work in advancing your cause. On the contrary, it can only make matters worse.

Here's what else can happen when you disassociate yourself from your emotions post-epiphany: rebound. While some research shows that heading quickly into a rebound relationship isn't always a bad thing as long as you know why you're doing it, rushing into rebound sex can be disastrous.

Consider that researchers at the University of Missouri asked 170 students who'd been through a breakup in the last eight months to keep a diary for three months chronicling their emotions, sexual activity, and motivation.[14] Of them, 59 percent said that they'd slept with someone new within the first month of their breakup; 35 percent had sex to get over their ex, and 25 percent had sex as a form of revenge. People who were dumped were especially likely to feel angry and distressed enough to seek out rebound sex as a way to distract themselves and get back at their exes.

While rebound sex may feel exciting in the moment, researchers at the City University of New York and the University of Illinois found it can also leave you feeling either more broken-hearted (since you're comparing it to sex with your ex, making you feel worse about the breakup) or more like you want to go back to your ex, but not for the right reasons.[15] They found that the short-term effect of rebound sex is often a feeling of emptiness and disempowerment, which can make the sting of heartbreak even worse.

Maxine, whom I mentioned in chapter 1, understands this firsthand. She'd been married and divorced three times from abusive and alcoholic men like her father. "I'd have one affair after the next, using sex with a new guy to help me survive one marriage or just get out, because I didn't want to deal with my feelings," she says.

It's only when she learned to slow down, process her reasons why, and stop searching for the validation she'd learned she needed, that she was able to open up to being with Everett. "I love Everett in a different way than I loved the others," she says. "Our relationship is so much more than sex. He's a super awesome human being who'd never be abusive in a million years. I can let my guard down with him. He loves me to death and I love him back . . . for all the right reasons this time." They've been happily married for ten years.

Not dealing with your feelings after an epiphany can also manifest in your going back to a flawed relationship, even when you know you shouldn't. Or it can take you out of the game altogether, like it did for Gabrielle, sixty-two, owner of a home cleaning service who lost her husband when she was just fifty. To avoid ever having to feel that kind of pain again, she realized she'd need to block herself off from love. So she did, for eleven years.

And then she ran into Steve, an old friend who was interested in her. "Even though Steve was a great guy and healthy, I just couldn't imagine losing someone else and going through that kind of suffering again," she said.

But Steve wouldn't take no for an answer. He showed up at her father's house on New Year's Eve with a rose for Gabrielle and her sister, and a tomato pie for her dad. They went for a walk and kissed, and that was it. "I listened to your TEDx talk and thought, *If she could do it, I could too.* Here I had a wonderful man right in front of me. But I wasn't letting him in. I decided to let go and take the chance." They just celebrated their three-year anniversary.

Here's another reason to face your feelings in the wake of an epiphany: because it's good for you. Research from Harvard

Medical School shows that the chronic stress from unresolved emotions can trigger your sympathetic nervous system's fight-or-flight response, slowing digestion, resulting in gas, bloating, constipation, vomiting, and even ulcers. Other studies show it can also increase your risk of heart disease.[16]

If having improved health and clarity isn't enough of a reason to deal with your feelings in the aftermath of epiphany, consider this: If you're mired down in unresolved emotion, how will you take the risks necessary to act boldly? And as you now know, when it comes to letting go, that's the ticket.

Do What's Counterintuitive

Many years ago, while I was writing for *Shape* magazine, I took Shaolin kung fu at a small dojo in Chicago as a way to collect fodder for my column. I'd also always wanted to try my hand at martial arts—it looked fun and useful, especially since I was a single woman living alone in the city.

My teacher, Sifu Dino, taught me a lot, but never more than he did on the day he got me down on the ground as part of a lesson in self-defense and asked me what I was going to do about the fact that I was on my back and he was sitting on my stomach, pretending to sucker punch me in the head and face.

I immediately started to push him off and away from my body, when he grabbed my arms and pinned me to the ground, leaving me virtually helpless. Never push away, he said. You give the attacker a longer range of motion to do you real damage. Instead, pull them in close. Not only will you have more ability to do them damage—knee them in the groin, put your fingers in their eyes, or bite them—but you'll also have the element of surprise on your side.

I know it's counterintuitive, he said, but it works.

I loved this and never forgot it because it's a powerful analogy for what I'm trying to help you do in this chapter. While your first instinct may be to push away the hard feelings in an attempt to protect yourself from further pain—as I did before Sophie and I got in the car that day to go home—resist. It's the wrong approach. Instead, pull your feelings in close. Let yourself be surprised by what you find, since there's gold in that surprise.

It's the stuff your subconscious has been hiding away that you absolutely need to know in order to make any necessary changes and move on with your life. Remind yourself that epiphany and the need to let go can hurt. Then prepare yourself to weather the storm.

Know that ignoring or suppressing the feelings and necessary self-examination to come will only prolong your agony and the grieving process. Healthy coping means knowing that you can't avoid the pain of loss, but you can push past it by going there . . . to the hard stuff.

This is your moment to get it all out. The afterglow of a powerful revelation is your golden opportunity to do an effective postmortem . . . on the relationship or the belief or whatever that epiphany told you it was time to let go of, because what you feel and, in turn, need to do will never be fresher or clearer in your mind.

This is your chance to look deeply at yourself and understand your own motivation. You can get there by asking yourself some important questions: Did you stay too long? Give too much? Let a limiting belief direct the show? Were your eyes open or closed to the truth? What role did you play? What actions do you feel led you to this outcome? And how do you feel about it all now? Are you mad at yourself? Pleased with yourself? Feeling that you could have done better or worse? Was any of it your fault? If so, what? Why do you think? And how do you feel about it? Can you forgive yourself for being human and imperfect? Do you even see it that way? If not, why not? How will you take your lessons so you can let go in a way that puts you on a better road?

The more questions, the better.

Do. The. Work.

Because here's the thing: as human beings, self-examination is in our DNA. And from a practical perspective, it will take you less time and energy to let your feelings out than to hold them in. Think Hoover Dam. The stomach flu. Your gut on Thanksgiving. Can you imagine if you tried to hold these things in and then went about the business of daily life? With the stomach flu? Instead, take control. Accept the reality of what is and do the work around it so you can move through the business of daily life without wondering when and if you're going to lose it, and that other shoe is going to drop.

Once you work through your feelings and understand your motivation for either staying in a relationship that wasn't right for you, hanging onto a belief that wasn't doing you justice, or attracting the same bad choices over and over again, you'll reap all kinds of benefits, including a happier love situation, more confidence, and better health to boot.

Consider that people who cope with their emotions constructively have a lower resting blood pressure than people with fewer coping skills. Psychologists at the Mount Sinai Medical Center in New York City measured participants' physiological responses after they were asked questions meant to spark irritation. People who scored high on a measure of constructive anger returned to their baseline blood pressure levels often within five minutes, while those who scored lower took up to ninety minutes to reduce their blood pressure.[17]

It's also healthier to embrace forgiveness on the other side of anger, once you've moved through all the other necessary emotions. I'm not just talking about forgiving another person but forgiving yourself for staying too long where you shouldn't, letting an errant belief guide the way, forgetting to listen to your own voice and instincts—you know, forgiveness as one of the ultimate and most critical acts of Big Wild Love. Now's the time to pull that rabbit out of your hat.

Especially when you reflect that it's been well documented by science that forgiveness lights the way for improved emotional and physical well-being. Consider that in one study alone, researchers at Hope College in Michigan recorded the psychophysiological and emotional responses, as well as facial expressions, of seventy participants who were asked to remember a time in which they were hurt or mistreated by someone else. Then they rehearsed being either (a) forgiving of that person by being empathetic and conciliatory, or (b) being unforgiving by rehearsing the hurt or holding a grudge. The results showed that forgiveness was associated with the healthiest profile.[18]

All of this is to say that when you're feeling the opposite—stressed and unforgiving—the best course of action is to work through it and go deep.

Joan, a fifty-two-year-old university professor, knows this all too well, after leaving her boyfriend of three years just before her fortieth birthday. Her boyfriend had an art business, and they were traveling to Paris for an art show where she thought he would finally propose to her. But he didn't. He worked the whole time. And she'd had enough.

Suddenly, instead of celebrating her new engagement, she found herself on her own, having an epiphany: that she would never come before his art business. Feeling sad and lonely and angry at herself for thinking it would all work out the way she wanted even though she'd seen signs to the contrary for months, she let go of him once they'd arrived home.

That's when she started asking herself a lot of questions about what happened, what she'd missed, and her part in all of it. "It was hard and wonderful to do that kind of examination. I had a lot of feelings to work through and a lot of questions to answer about why I stayed, but the experience of doing so served me a lot." She ultimately came to forgive herself for not leaving sooner, a necessary step in her evolving journey to find love.

Here's what else she learned:

- What wasn't negotiable for her.
- That she wanted someone who'd done as much internal work as she had.
- That when people tell you something about themselves early or even later in a relationship, to believe them.
- Not to make excuses for other people's brokenness.
- That no matter what happened in a relationship—and life—she'd be OK.
- That with or without him, she could and would be a whole and happy person.

"When we broke up, I had no idea what the future held," she says, now married to someone else. "But I was grounded in reality. And you know what? Letting go didn't kill me. To the contrary, I'm still here and doing just fine."

Getting through the Muck

I love Joan's story. And Gabrielle's. And Maxine's. And all the stories. Because they illustrate how possible it is to get on the other side of your emotions. So how do you do it? Move through your post-epiphany moment with grace and aplomb?

I have some ideas.

Here are four, in particular, for helping you get it done. Pull out your belief journal or whatever you're using to scribe, and let's get down to it. Read through each idea and then work your way through the exercises. You can create your own daylong detox or take each idea in bite-sized chunks. Either way works. If you take the latter approach, I suggest doing one idea a day for four days in a week, or one idea a week for four weeks. Whatever your appetite and schedule allow.

However you do it, know that the objective is to get you to dive more deeply and productively into your emotions so you can understand them and yourself, and then release them.

#1: *Forgive yourself.*

While we touched on this in chapter 1 as an integral part of cultivating Big Wild Love, it bears repeating and focusing on here because some of the stuff that may come up for you as part of your self-examination could reignite old feelings, wounds, and moments of self-loathing. Forgive as necessary.

You may start this process—of post-epiphany self-evaluation—believing you have nothing to forgive yourself for. And that may very well be the case, but probably not. What I've found in talking with other women and even from my own experience is that what starts as anger, for example, at another person or circumstance, often finds its way back to us being mad at ourselves. It's classic, once we've spent some time evaluating an epiphany, this wanting to beat ourselves up: for staying, making a mistake, not knowing, knowing and not doing, believing something "stupid," being imperfect, thinking it would happen or could never happen, you name it. This is where forgiveness comes in.

You must open your heart to the most important person in your life—YOU. If you don't, how will you ever move forward with compassion, clarity, and the ability to forgive others who are worthy? Start with the person in the mirror. Forgive yourself . . . for whatever you uncover in your emotional due diligence. For whatever lessons you didn't take in the past or allow yourself to see. For wherever you've been imperfect. For misstepping. For being confused. For a wayward belief. For not loving yourself. For whatever comes out of the process of self-exploration as a result of that epiphany. You have time to make good on all of it.

Start by realizing that, at the time, you made the best decisions possible for yourself and all those involved in your situation. You did the best you could with what you had. Allow yourself to witness what you think you need to be forgiven for, as an observer, so you can see it more objectively and take away the appropriate lessons without having your thinking muddied by emotion. Talk it through with a trusted friend or mentor or counselor to help keep things in perspective. Remember, you don't have to be perfect to be loved or in a healthy relationship.

And last but not least, forgive yourself as a priority. You're only human.

Exercise:

Answer the following questions:

- What do I need to forgive the other person in my current situation for?
- What do I need to forgive myself for? Today? In the past?
- How can I do both realistically and lovingly? (Remember the tips I mentioned to help you above!)

#2: *Sort through your feelings.*

While processing a breakup or a belief or whatever you need to let go of doesn't always feel good, organizing your emotions around it can give you context. And that's powerful in terms of gaining the self-knowledge, courage, and confidence you need to act boldly for what you want so you can get closer to having them the next time. Here are some things to think about as you sort through your feelings.

Prepare yourself for the fact that having an epiphany that leads to a breakup may leave you feeling like a heroin addict looking for her next fix. It can be that intense. That's because falling in love triggers a rush of hormones that activate the brain's reward system.[19] So even if you initiated the breakup for good reason, you could still physically feel like an addict suffering from withdrawal.

You may also find yourself grappling with self-blame, thinking you were the reason or the cause for whatever went wrong. But let go of taking it personally. That's not productive. And besides, while whatever may have happened affected you, it's rarely, if ever, about you. Or what you did wrong.

And even if, for shits and giggles, it was? That doesn't mean you had ill will or malice at heart. So let yourself off the hook. Instead, focus on what you need to learn from the experience. Take notes so you can adjust your approach going forward.

Exercise:
Create a chart with five columns. In it, you're going to lay out your concerns post-epiphany, your associated feelings, and what, if anything, you can do about it, so you can see that you're not as helpless as you may feel. Here's an example of how it could look:

What problem do I have in my life?	How does it make me feel?	Can I control this problem?
I don't deserve love.	Sad, lonely, despondent, hopeless	Yes
I never meet anybody.	Sad and depressed	Yes
My ex lied to me several times.	Pissed off at him and myself because I stayed anyway	No—I have no control over whether my ex is telling the truth or not. Only what I do once I find out about it.
My ex has a new girlfriend.	Heartbroken	No
My husband chews with his mouth open after having dental work.	Irritated	Probably not, especially if he does it because he's in pain
Most of my boyfriends have talked down to me, and, while I don't like it, I still accept it and stay with them.	Confused, unclear, bad, afraid, angry, untrusting, self loathing	Yes

What can I do?	What do I need to learn from it?
Identify my limiting beliefs either with or without the help of a trained counselor and work to create change that leads me to believe I do deserve healthy love.	That it's a likely culprit in keeping me from having the relationship I want.
Seek help of a therapist, talk to a dating coach, work on cultivating Big Wild Love, etc.	That it's only true if I use the belief to create a self-fulfilling prophecy. But I have other choices.
Let go of ex, work on Big Wild Love, forgive myself.	That I may be ignoring or missing the red flags in relationships or my choices need to get better.
Move on, unfollow from social media, disconnect for a while from shared friends, etc.	That exes move on and that I should too. And to get help if I'm struggling with that. To also make sure that I don't take his/her moving on as a sign that there's something wrong with me.
Love him anyway, scream into a pillow, ignore it.	That my husband is human and imperfect. And needs more dental work.
Identify this as a limiting belief and work to change it, tell partner how you feel and let go as needed, etc.	That I have a limiting belief I need to uncover and eliminate, and then replace it with a new more empowering belief. I also need to work on cultivating more Big Wild Love.

Exercise:

If you miss being with someone, something about your current relationship, or just being by yourself, write a letter to yourself or the other person laying out what you miss. The point of this exercise is to gain the wisdom that you don't need anybody or to be needed to be whole.

#3: Be prepared to reinvent yourself.

Or at least parts of yourself, as needed. Often when we're sorting through our feelings after an epiphany, we're left with a sense of not only "Where do we go from here?" but also "Who are we?" That's especially potent coming off of a long-term relationship, where research shows our identity can become intertwined with another person's. In fact, the longer we're with someone, the more we share what some call an "interpersonal cognitive system," whereby each person relies on the other to fill in certain memory gaps. With this in mind, it's no wonder that breaking up with someone you've been with for a while can feel as traumatic as losing an arm. I can personally attest to this fact.

I remember seeing an old friend years after I'd let go of Hector. I was with someone else, and she looked confused and uncomfortable. Finally, I asked her, "Is it weird to see me with someone other than Hector?" And she said, "Oh my gosh, it's just bizarre. I have to get used to it!"

If *she* had to get used to it, can you imagine how I felt?

I had to reinvent myself after leaving a relationship of twelve years, and, regardless of how long you were stuck in your situation and what that post-epiphany process led you to, you'll likely have to do all or some of the same.

Now's your chance to not only be organically yourself but also be strategic in terms of setting your aspirations. Who do you want to be? What habits and behaviors would you like to reimagine? How can you take this opportunity to go to the next level of who you really are? I'm not saying you should copy another person's style or personality—that would be impossible anyway. But you will likely have to find a way to disassociate from what you've left behind and recreate something newer and fresher in its place.

And while you may perceive that as being hard work, or grieve over the loss of the parts of yourself you've left behind (which is valid, and you should do that), there's also another side to it. If the relationship or situation you came out of didn't enhance your life or help you grow as a person, then leaving it behind and reimagining yourself is actually a good thing.

Consider that researchers at Monmouth University in New Jersey studied 155 participants who'd experienced a breakup within the past six months, and found that leaving a stagnant relationship actually freed them to rediscover more of what and whom they wanted to be, and increased their positive emotions.[20]

There are a lot of ways to rethink yourself and your life in the wake of whatever led you to that epiphany. Start by exploring what makes you happy, especially if you haven't engaged in certain activities or experiences because a significant other wasn't interested. Try stuff you've always wanted to try but never did because of an unwilling partner or limiting belief. Realign empowering beliefs to more aggressive, new goals. Be open to new experiences. Say yes. Shake things up. Take risks. Befriend people who have lives, relationships, and belief systems you admire. Embrace new ideas and opportunities, especially if they thrill you and scare you—to me, that's the perfect reason why you should.

It's also important to clear out of your mind, heart, and life that which no longer serves, including any connections to people, places, or things that don't make you feel good.

Exercise:

To get you thinking about who you are as a whole person, irrespective of anybody else, write your thoughts after each of the following prompts. As you do, consider them in the context of love, family, spirituality, money, work, and health.

I am . . .

I'd like to try . . .

I always wanted to . . .

I'm excited to . . .

My goal is to . . .

I'd like to be friends with someone who is . . .

My ex never wanted to . . . but I did.

#4: Focus on the positive.

While you'll undoubtedly spend a lot of time working through the negative aspects of creating change as a result of your epiphany, it's equally important to focus on the positive aspects of that epiphany as well and where it has the potential to lead you. Ask yourself: What good has come from it? Then list it out. Are you now working with a more empowering belief system? Able to see a future, where you couldn't before? Free of someone who was controlling you in a way that felt toxic? Open to dream and believe there are better things waiting on the horizon?

What is it?

"Our thoughts are pure energy," says Susan Apollon. "If we continue to focus on what brings us down, on the person or situation that causes us pain, we will only have more pain. But if we choose to focus on that which brings us joy, we can begin to vibrate at a higher level. And that will bring us more of what we want."

If you're struggling to find the good in your new post-epiphany world, the journal exercise highlighted next will help, especially when you consider that writing is great for gaining a more positive perspective. I know we've been doing a lot of it in our work together, but doing it here is especially powerful . . . and backed up by research.

In one study, researchers at Monmouth University in New Jersey asked eighty-seven single people (twenty-five male and six-ty-two female) who'd recently been through a breakup to write about their deepest thoughts and feelings about what led up to it and how they felt a few days and weeks after. Participants were then assigned to one of three writing groups: negatively focused, positively focused, and neutral. The positively focused group experienced an increase in positive emotions, while the other groups stayed the same.[21]

Exercise:
Not surprisingly, this one is a journal prompt that asks you to write out your answers to the following questions:

- What are the positive aspects of your epiphany and its consequences, and how do they make you feel?
- List at least five positive aspects.
- And then write at least three full pages in your journal (e.g., front, back, and then front) for each positive aspect you come up with. Keep your hand moving.

Lastly, as you move through this post-epiphany process, continue on the path of Big Wild Love by using any one of these prompts as a way to go deeper. Remind yourself that while some of the work you'll do here may push you to a place of discomfort, you have everything you need inside of yourself to not only sur-vive it but also thrive in its aftermath.

The goal is to acknowledge your feelings so you can let them go. And go back out into your relationship or the world of dating with a clean slate.

How will you know when you're ready?

A lot will depend on your situation, personality, and how well you've gotten through any emotional roadblocks. While some studies have attempted to identify the exact length of time it takes to recover from a breakup, one suggests three months, another says eleven months, and another says seventeen months and twenty-six days. You see where I'm going here? There is no magic number.

You'll know your work is done when you feel at peace. When the current and original sources of pain—issues that you thought you'd long let go of but that came up again as part of your intro-spection—are healed. When you can bring a person or situation up and there's no more hurt feelings. You don't feel angry or sad or have the desire to hit back.

"You'll know when there's been a healing," says Apollon. "There will be a rebalancing of energy and you'll feel it."

That's when you'll be ready. To move on.

Moving Forward after a Clearing

By the time I'd gotten to the third and final break in Hector's and my relationship—and that last powerful epiphany, the one I could no longer ignore—I knew what I had to do. And I did it.

I grieved that loss like a championship fighter. Crawled into the agony. I threw things (although never furniture). Analyzed the situation and my role in it until I wanted to vomit. Anesthetized myself with pizza. Watched Lifetime television until I started thinking the characters were real people, at which point I checked myself. Asked myself why, over and over and over again, while crying some more, whale-like noises coming out of my voice box the likes of which I'd never heard before (thank goodness I had neighbors to make sure I wasn't choking). I played the victim. Then I played the warrior. Then the victim again. *I hated them and I'd show them.* Back and forth I went, like a child of divorce. I made pretend I was twenty years younger and twenty years older, asking myself how I got where I was and how it would all turn out for me. I swam through my thoughts and feelings with vigor and tenacity, like Diana Nyad swimming her way through the dark and vast Atlantic Ocean, sans the lip balm. I was tireless, fearless, and indulgent. After all, what did I have to lose that I hadn't lost already? I reminded myself over and over again of that line Matthew Broderick says in the movie *The Freshman*: "There's a kind of freedom in being completely screwed . . . because you know things can't get worse."

It was incredibly freeing. That's the beauty of the aftermath. Beyond those raw and inflamed nerve endings comes a wondrous regrowth—of resilience and fortitude and veracity. There's the light. The freedom. The hope and possibility that come from making it all the way through the journey with all limbs intact. Making it to the epiphany was milestone enough. But surviving the epiphany? Well, that was me getting a crown and a sash, and taking my first walk down the runway.

I finally had the courage and confidence to ask the questions I'd avoided for more than a decade, for fear the answers would set me up for a lifetime of anger, self-loathing, and regret. Why had I chosen Hector? Why did I stay so long? What did I get from it? What did it cost me? How could I let go so I didn't make the same mistakes and choices the next time? Did I even believe there would be a next time? It would be the answers to these questions, no longer muddied by emotion, that would allow me to make

better choices in the spirit of what was possible from a new relationship—and not from a wounded place, where love had failed
me on so many counts.

I was now officially a survivor. That epiphany didn't get me.
I got myself . . . back. And even better. Because I was actually
looking at myself for the first time in a long time.

Now I was free to imagine what came next. To apply the
answers to the questions I'd asked myself so bravely during that
sometimes enlightening, sometimes freeing, sometimes harrow-
ing postmortem, post-epiphany.

What did I want from love? It was a question I hadn't dared
to ask for a long time. But now, well, I was ready.

Chapter 6

THE END GOAL

I wanted to be my own lotus flower.

—V, 55, California

One day I was taking Sophie for our morning walk. It was after that second break in my relationship with Hector, just before we got back together a few months later. As Sophie investigated a patch of grass just outside my apartment building, I had a come-to-Jesus moment. I asked myself a simple question: What do I want? From love and even life?

After all, I did not enjoy melting down on the side of the highway, as I had that day when I went to pick up Sophie and she didn't want to come home with me. And as it would turn out, I didn't enjoy life without Hector either. I missed him so much that I started to rethink things in an attempt to figure out how we could stay together.

Maybe I could live without marriage—maybe it didn't have to be a deal breaker. If Hector and I could forge a new agreement around what commitment looked like, maybe we could meet somewhere in the middle. And stay together.

After all, we loved each other. That much I knew. And we didn't see other people, so on some level, we were committed—even if we didn't live together or have a legally binding certificate as proof. What difference would a certificate make anyway? I had two from my undergraduate and graduate studies, and I had no idea where they even were. So how important could that piece of paper be?

If Hector and I could figure out a way to be together that satisfied both of our criteria for feeling happy and grounded, perhaps we could be OK. Get through this.

As Sophie did her business, I conducted some of my own: I decided to open my mind to the options I'd been unwilling to entertain. I began to ask myself, in the mirror, how I would feel if I never got married. Sad, but, you know, I could get over it. I'd learn to accept what was. After all, we humans adapt to anything. I mean, look at all those hostages who've survived captivity in other countries. They come home and, after some time, they're fine—sure, they have some issues, but they're mostly grateful to be alive.

Not that I was in captivity, but I had felt trapped in a damned-if-you-do-and-damned-if-you-don't situation for some time. And yet were things really that dramatic? Was I really without any range of motion? A lot of people don't get married. And they're happy. I had a good man who loved me. I'd be crazy to let go of him.

Besides, that stint on the side of the highway sent me the very clear message: not yet. It wasn't time to say goodbye. Perhaps

I hadn't tried everything I could to be happy inside of our relationship. I'd take marriage off the table and everything would be fine. Hector and I would reconnect around the simple joy of just being together. Our relationship deserved that chance.

I was excited about this new approach and reached out to Hector to talk about getting back together. Told him I was open to moving forward without the promise of a ring and a wedding, to which he said this: "Jilly, that's great. I love you, girl."

And then, this: ". . . and hey, you never know what the future has to bring."

There it was. The words that I knew he spoke so innocently, without malice or manipulation, but which kept me on the hook for years. And sure, you don't ever know. Although I did know, for years, in my gut, but I just didn't want to listen.

But it would remind me . . .

About three weeks after reuniting, Hector and I decided to meet for lunch at a favorite restaurant in the city. It was an unusually warm and windy Saturday in January. The skies were overcast and the air definitely smelled like rain. Despite the seventy-eight-degree temps, it felt almost ominous.

I was restless.

When we arrived at the restaurant, the hostess sat us in a room full of couples, nary a single or threesome in sight. I don't usually pay attention to those sorts of things, but for some reason on that day, I couldn't miss it. They could have been brothers and sisters, work colleagues, or cheating lovers—it didn't matter. As I scanned each pair, I realized something.

I wanted to get married. I couldn't let it go.

I projected onto those couples the fantasy of what I didn't have with Hector. They were all blissfully married, grateful to have found one another.

Even though I knew it was crazy to impose my fairy tale onto a group of strangers, I had woken up thinking about how absurd it felt to have to set a time and day to see someone I'd been with for more than a decade. And rather than feel more settled when the two of us sat down, it suddenly got worse.

I looked at Hector, immersed in the menu, unaware of my growing anger and frustration, and took a large gulp of water. Feeling my stare, he finally looked up and smiled.

"Hey, want to share something?" That smile was a killer.

"Sure, how about a life?"

"Wait, what?" he said. "I thought we talked about this . . . we agreed . . ."

He was right. We had talked about it . . . over and over and over and over and over and over. And the outcome of our conversations never changed, along with our relationship.

The only way through this impasse was to start asking a different question. Instead of whether he'd ever marry me, to which I already knew the answer, I needed to ask myself why I was waiting for him to decide my future.

After all, wasn't my life up to me?

It was a question I had never asked in any of the many relationships I'd had over the years. I'd always waited for the other person to do their thing. Then I'd just comply. Figure out how to survive in the wake of another person's actions. I'd deal with it. Overcome it. Rise above it. Mourn it. Move past it. Whatever I had to do to get by—except, as it turns out, figure out what I actually wanted.

My job was never to be proactive or take my own actions around what I wanted or how I'd even get it, but instead to remain braced for impact. And keep my expectations low.

It never occurred to me that anything was in my hands, the least of which was whether someone stayed or left, including myself. That I could, at any given point in time, simply choose to pick up my toys and go home. Because I never fully took the time to assess where precisely home was. Which was one of the reasons why I consistently found myself stuck in places I didn't want to be, beholden to the whims and proclivities of other people instead of deciding where I belonged for myself.

I had never been the least bit strategic about what I wanted. Never gotten deep, real, or serious about figuring it out. I just assumed that I'd know where home was—what I wanted—when I saw it. And that's how I lived and loved.

Impulsively and in the moment.

I left not only the end goal, but *my* end goal, up to chance, simply by never knowing what it was. Or doing the work necessary to figure it out.

And now here I was. In my forties, twelve years into a relationship and still confused about what came next. Because if I couldn't get Hector to marry me (and none of us can get anybody to do anything they don't want to do), what then?

(I had no clue.)

What did I want?

(No clue.)

And if I didn't know what I wanted, how would I ever get there?

(I wouldn't.)

The next step in my evolution of letting go was clear: answer the question.

Do You Have Romanticitis Disconnecteditis?

In Dan Slater's *Love in the Time of Algorithms: What Technology Does to Meeting and Mating,* he points out how the first online dating services tried to find matches for their clients based almost exclusively on what they said, in a questionnaire, they wanted in a partner.[22] But it didn't work. Then Match.com hired a researcher who tried to figure out why a lot of the couples that the site's algorithm said were a perfect fit didn't make it past the first date. They learned that the kind of partner people said they wanted didn't match up with the kind of partner they were actually interested in.

Well, this is a problem. And not just for those of us seeking a mate on Match.com, but for anybody who's looking for love unsuccessfully. Because if you're approaching it saying you want one thing but are actually going for another, watch out. Danger Will Robinson, hold onto your hat, and grab your favorite yoga pants for security . . . finding your way to healthy love is going to be a wild and wonky ride.

Because you'll never find what you want from love if you suffer from what I suspect the folks on Match.com did—Romanticitis Disconnecteditis. A potentially chronic condition that has (a) yes, a name I made up, and (b) the power to keep us acutely divided between what we *think* or *say* we want versus what we actually *do* want in love.

Think about it logically: if we don't know what we want from love and how it fits into the broader picture of our lives, how will we ever get it? Luck? Osmosis? Divine intervention? It's like leaving the house without a destination in mind. Oh sure, we might wind up someplace interesting by happenstance or despite ourselves, but more than likely we'll find ourselves roaming the streets with blisters inflating like little bouncy houses on our feet. Walking in pain, wondering how we arrived at where we didn't want to go and searching for the quickest way out of there.

And yet according to research done by leadership specialist and coach Tracey Carr, less than one person in every hundred actually knows what they want.[23] As a result, she and others agree, most people wind up arriving at a destination they didn't want or choose consciously.

I can certainly attest to that. By the time I'd arrived at my come-to-Jesus moment walking the dog, it was clear that I hadn't really thought seriously about wanting marriage because I was too willing to forego it. Saying I didn't want it—that I'd be OK with a different solution, like just agreeing to be together forever—was my attempt to distract myself from the blistering pain of my own situation and convince myself that everything was just fine.

In retrospect, I can see now that I had a pretty good case of Romanticitis Disconnecteditis, brought on by limiting beliefs. They had me in a bind—too afraid to make a move, not believing that I deserved the love I wanted or that it was out there for me, not wanting to go through the heartbreak of leaving or taking a chance and finding anyone else, not thinking I could survive the loss of Hector, assuming I was sure to wind up alone.

To cultivate the BWL I needed, I had to be brave.

Asking myself what I truly wanted—from a partner, love, and relationship—could have saved me a lot of time and anxiety. But instead, I let the safety of settling and short-term gratification rule the roost, as I suspect they did for some of Match.com's users, and definitely for many of the women I've interviewed.

These women turned a blind eye as a way to avoid the change they simply weren't ready to create. Knowing what they wanted—even asking the question more deeply, beyond just what they had in the moment—would have shone an unwelcome light on the subject of where they were at in love. Reminded them of what they lacked and the limiting beliefs they weren't ready to address.

These women were used to deferring their wants and needs—it's what they'd been doing for years or watched their parents do—and didn't understand or see the value of this type of self-examination. Beyond accepting, of course, the physiological low-hanging fruit of wanting sex and not wanting to be alone.

They'd also convinced themselves that luck and chemistry played an important role in finding and sustaining love. That being too thoughtful about whom they dated and how would just interrupt the spontaneity of romance.

Or they'd made themselves hellbent on finding a soul mate, which, of course, set them up for failure. And I say "of course" because I don't believe a soul mate is a thing. To me, looking for one is reaching for the unreachable. A great excuse for playing it safe, whether staying in an already bad situation, never leaving the house, eschewing dating altogether, or being perfectly OK with cuddling up with Netflix.

Mind you, I'm coming from a place of practicality here and not bitterness.

Because finding and maintaining healthy love is incredibly accessible. It's true as an enterprise of both the heart and the mind. It's not about any magic spells or formulas that align the stars just so, setting you on a path for meeting that one and only person in the world made just for you. If you're betting on a unicorn like that, you're setting yourself up for disappointment and potentially worse.

Science backs me up here. There's a lot of evidence that shows how looking at prospects through the lens of finding a soul mate is more likely to have you making bad relationship choices than actually finding that one special, haloed person. Like, for example, rushing into situations that fizzle out quickly or jumping ship at the first sign of conflict.

This is just one of many downsides to going into love and relationships blind or with unrealistic expectations, without having gone through the exercise of deciding what you want from love, beyond just the moment.

A few other downsides:

You take whomever you can get, latching onto the first person who shows you any attention, even if it's negative.

You go into a relationship without focus, impulse-shopping on dating websites, and casting aside what you really want for something or someone who seems better or more attractive in the moment.

You guesstimate your next move, following dating trends that are misguided (remember *The Rules*, which had women play dating games to snag a guy they probably wouldn't want anyway because he'd be into the thrill of the chase and not necessarily them? Yep, me too . . .), fixating on what you're not getting, dissatisfied with what you have, unable to see how things could work out, confused about how to forge ahead, making choices that aren't in your best interests, and searching for something that might or might not exist or meet your criteria for healthy love over the long haul.

Sounds exhausting, doesn't it?

There is a better way. And it's free, available, supremely doable, and all about you!

Keep reading.

Knowing the End Goal Is the Cure

There's a surefire way to prevent yourself from coming down with a case of Romanticitis Disconnecteditis. It's knowing with strategy, clarity, and purpose what you want from love, generating a thoughtful and tangible end goal that you can realistically achieve. Because when you do, it becomes very easy to assess whether your current situation will get you there.

Or not so much.

And if you think terms like *end goal* and *strategy* should be mainly reserved for the boardroom, I firmly and respectfully disagree. On the contrary, we have much to learn from the world of business when it comes to knowing what we want and actually getting it—yes, even in love. Because love isn't just about the aforementioned unicorns, valentines, angels, and roses; seeing it as such is part of the problem. It's about both our hearts and our brains.

Consider that business leaders take a more realistic approach—at least the ones who are successful—toward getting where they want to go, in that there's no way they'd engage in the bull crap so many do when it comes to dating, romance, and relationships.

Can you imagine those business leaders negotiating with themselves for less money? Less control? Less brand loyalty? Or hiring people who are mysterious, unreliable, aloof, uncommitted, poor communicators, and who are less interested in advancing the company than they are in advancing themselves?

Companies put a very high priority on knowing what they want and whom, and what they need to align themselves with to get there, and the same should hold true for anybody looking for healthy, productive love.

While companies' endgame is money, your endgame is [fill in the blank]. (See how I did that?)

In their case and in yours, strategy doesn't just apply, it's critical. Especially when you talk about setting goals, assessing risk, identifying the how, and letting go for results.

It is, in fact, a similar type of deep strategic work that will do the job on all counts. That will allow us to discern what we want—using not just our hearts, guts, and hopes for the best, but effective planning and our intellect.

That's the real gold in those hills.

Just ask Terri, a successful executive who, at age twenty-five, thought she wanted marriage with a man even though she was secretly attracted to women. She married William because that was what her family and church wanted. And she tried to convince herself she wanted it too.

"Three weeks after my honeymoon, Alice and I met at work," says Terri, now forty-two. "I didn't want to like her in the worst way. I wanted to love my husband."

So Terri stayed focused. She worked hard to convince herself she was happy where she was, deferring her needs for Will's, until he told her on their third Christmas together that they couldn't put a tree up in their house. He said he didn't want one, although Terri never fully understood the reason.

"Christmas was a big deal when I was growing up. We always had a tree and a lot of decorations. That was a very happy memory. Taking away the tree was taking away a huge part of me; it was also a huge wake-up call," she says, surmising that he did it to force change, since he knew she wasn't all in.

That's when she realized how much she was sacrificing to be with him, and how she wasn't making anybody happy by doing so—by forfeiting her own wants and needs to appease other people. "I wanted a Christmas tree with all the trimmings. I wanted the freedom to be my true self.

"I wanted to be with Alice."

Terri knew what she wanted but was afraid to name it because she was holding onto a limiting belief that told her other people came first.

She was also afraid that if she named what she wanted, she'd have to upend everything to get it. And there were no guarantees it would all work out. Couldn't she just keep going and find a way to be happy with Will?

The answer was no. In fact, few if any can exist peacefully inside a life that doesn't fit. And you shouldn't have to. Not if you're big wild loving.

Terri ultimately got there—decided on what she wanted (end goal) and how she'd get at it (strategy)—and left her marriage as a result. And today, she and Alice have been happily married for fifteen years.

Terri's story is illustrative of what can happen when you don't name what you want and go for it. You waste time. You hurt yourself and oftentimes others.

You get stuck.

Instead, ramp up your BWL so you can name and then proudly claim, without hesitation or looking over your shoulder, what you want. Because without it, you're nowhere you want to be. Trust me.

That means going deep to find and then rid yourself of the limiting beliefs that tell you what you want isn't possible. Listening to your gut, because you know it's the truth inside of you trying desperately to get your attention. Letting your own voice rise above all the others clamoring for real estate in your brain.

Be willing to feel the pain of change and do it anyway, despite the blisters begging you to stay put. Be proud of what you want, believe you can get it, and don't stop until you're there.

Bringing Your Vision to Life

So now let's talk about how to figure out what you want. Before I get down to brass tacks, I need to make an important distinction between knowing what you want and choosing what you want from a predetermined set of options (which we'll talk more about in the next chapter in terms of how to identify and choose options for getting to your end goal).

Knowing has you coming from an internal space—making a decision about the "what" that leaves you feeling fulfilled, is aligned with your values, and is reflective of your unique set of preferences, biases, worldview, beliefs, and experiences, irrespective of the options on the table for "how."

But *choosing* merely has you coming from an external place of picking off of a list.

The difference between these two is the difference between an essay and a multiple-choice question. I want you to come to what you want from a place of original thought. To do the former. Here's an example to help you see how this could work in practice.

Let's say you want a hamburger. It's been a while and you know where to get a healthy, grass-fed version. So why not? You arrive at the restaurant hungry. Reviewing the menu, you suddenly find yourself attracted to a few other options—that Cobb salad looks good, and chicken and ribs, yum. Sure, you came in for a burger, but now that you're in the moment . . . you go for the ribs. And they're delicious, but you're still craving a burger once you're back at home. In this case, it would be easy enough to have it, but in love and relationships, not so much. The point being this: when you're thinking about an end goal, consider long-term satisfaction over instant gratification. And choose with intention.

OK, moving on . . . here are a few exercises to get you started navigating your way through that heart- and brain-space of *knowing*. They're great to do on a leisurely Saturday morning, after a nice walk, with a steaming mug of [insert beverage]. All you'll need is something to write with and your journal. And no multitasking. Turn off the phone and log out of Facebook. This is important work that really can change your life. So please, focus.

Exercise #1: Chart it out

Create a chart with three columns outlining what you want from love, what you don't want, and what you have currently in different areas of importance to you. In each horizontal row, write down five things only, since science says if you focus on too many at once, you won't be successful.

Here's a sample chart to give you an idea of what I'm talking about; in the first row, I even give you prompts to jog your thinking. Populate your chart so it reflects your thoughts, beliefs, desires, and experiences. Take the time you need to be thoughtful. And for more guidance, check out the caveats that follow it.

Ask Yourself:	What do I want from love?	What don't I want from love?	What do I have now?
Notes:	This can be regarding a partner, a relationship, or an end goal in general.	This doesn't have to relate to or be the converse of the previous column, unless that's how you truly feel—it can stand on its own.	If you're single or not in a relationship at the moment, consider using the prompts, "I have . . . the desire for, the opportunity to, the regret about, the wish I could, the hope that, the possibility of . . ."
1.	A partner who wants what I do, which is [marriage, not marriage, living together, long-term dating, stability, financial security, travel, etc.].	A partner who isn't sure what they want from a relationship.	A partner who swears he wants the commitment I do but gets mad, changes the subject, or goes home whenever I bring up the subject of marriage.

Ask Yourself:	What do I want from love?	What don't I want from love?	What do I have now?
2.	Someone who values and champions a partner like me who's [independent, successful, a homebody, an introvert, an extrovert, ambitious, financially secure, insecure, growth minded, etc.].	A partner who doesn't place a high value on good health and personal and professional growth.	A relationship that's comfortable but boring.
3.	Someone who has their own [hopes, dreams, money, kids, etc.] that I can [support, champion, love, share, etc.].	Drama.	The opportunity to attract a suitable partner who will embrace my professional success without feeling threatened.
4.	Someone who already has [children, money, security, a career path, etc.] and values [family, love, money, security, health, longevity, etc.].	Someone looking to piggyback on what I have and not contribute to or participate in a healthy and complete way to the relationship.	A partner that takes care of me financially, something I'm not able to do on my own, and which is important to me.
5.	Someone who places high importance on [healthy love, communication, etc.] and knows how to [give and receive love, share their thoughts and feelings freely, talk about problems, listen, etc.] in the spirit of [harmony, longevity, etc.].	Someone who's always been married, in a relationship, or part of a couple and doesn't know how to be alone.	Time to enjoy my single life and figure out who I am and what I want so I can create a plan for getting it.

Some caveats:

- Be specific. Studies have shown that goals are easier to reach if they're specific. For example, if family is important to you, write it as "I want to be with someone who is close to their parents and siblings, and who wants kids/ has kids, etc."
- Focus on the deeper aspects of what you want. Instead of focusing on how someone looks, consider their values, goals, desires.
- Get real about what you want, and not what you think you should want as a result of anybody else's input. There's no one right or wrong way to be in a relationship. Just be honest with yourself.
- Be realistic. I wanted to marry Hector, but it was obvious it wasn't going to happen. So, while you may want to have a meaningful relationship with George Clooney, well, you know . . .

Exercise #2: Write it out

As you're working through the chart, populating each cell, notice how each response makes you feel in your body. Does it make you feel anxious? Happy? Excited? Like you want to cry?

Review what you've written for any patterns in thought. Do you find one idea or goal stands out more than another? For example, do you talk a lot about family throughout? Work? Success? Travel? Look for trends. Pay close attention to what's coming up, and then journal about it. Here are some questions to get you started:

- How did I feel while writing in the chart? Where did I feel good? Bad? Sad? Etc.
- What are the major themes showing themselves in the chart?
- Why do I think they're coming up?

- Do they come from a place of positivity or negativity, of hope or pain?
- How do my current state and my desired future state sync up?
- How do I feel about that?
- What have I learned about myself and what I want as a result of this exercise?
- Am I willing to take action on those lessons?
- What am I willing to give up—and what is most important for me?
- If I had to choose three attributes, based on this work, that are most important to me in love (e.g., a partner and/or relationship), what would they be?

Exercise #3: Deciding versus choosing

Building on the opening point about knowing and not choosing, and using what you've discovered during the previous two exercises, complete the following exercise (based on your relationship status).

If you're in dating mode: Write down what you want on a piece of paper, including the type of partner, and tape it to the computer so you can see it. Then go onto a dating website and look at who's out there. Browse the lists of people that come up and consider who meets your preset criteria (versus winking at someone or choosing them just because you think they're cute or they remind you of someone you used to know or appeal to some limiting belief you haven't yet dealt with and has gotten you into trouble in a previous relationship). What do they have to offer from the perspective of your morals, values, likes, dislikes, goals, etc., at least as far as you can ascertain from their profile? Keep looking back at the paper with your end goal on it for guidance and notice how coming from a place of knowing versus choosing informs your choices. Are the choices you'd make from a place of knowing the same as the choices you'd make from a place of choosing? Are you choosing based on your end goal or a less thoughtful impulse? Journal around the answer.

If you're in relationship mode: Write down what you want on a clean piece of paper. Then hold it up to your current situation. Are they aligned? Out of alignment? Is what you say you want the same as what you have, or different? Journal around the answer, how you feel about it, and what action steps, if any, you're ready to take as a result.

Exercise #4: Create a vision board

Now that you've worked through the idea of what you want using words, it's time to build on that work by adding images. Create a vision board around the idea of what you want most from love. By adding mental pictures and images to the equation, you'll be integrating both parts of your brain to expand your thinking about what you truly want in life.

"I always tell my students that I collaged my husband into being," says Joan Cantwell, an expressive arts teacher. She wound up marrying for the first time at age forty-eight, using a vision board to home in on the qualities that were most important to her. "I wanted someone who had taken care of themselves, who had done a lot of internal work around who they were, and who not only knew what they wanted, but was ready for it . . . and me," she says, adding that it's important to focus on the internal and not external qualities that make somebody attractive to you. "I wanted a partner who'd already addressed their own issues and had moved on. Who knew how to be with women. And I got all of it."

She and others agree that creating a vision board that ultimately helps you manifest what and whom you want is not magic. Rather, it's a process that works if you do it correctly.

And I agree as well.

Before you get started, I do *not* recommend doing a vision board with a group of other people or at a party because I see it as intimate and important inner work that requires you to be focused and thoughtful. With that in mind, I suggest finding a time when you can be alone, quiet, and contemplative—and in a space of imagining freely (so don't do it after you've just gotten bad news or any other time when your emotions are charged or skewed toward the negative). You want to come from a positive and hopeful place.

Once there, it's simply a matter of following three easy steps:

1. Inventory. Cut out words and images from magazines and other places that really speak to you or tug at something inside of you, images that reflect what it is you want from love, partnership, and a relationship in particular. Imagine what these images are on their own and then inside the context of your broader life—and how that also might need to change or be reflected on the board.

Pull out anything that speaks to you and says, "Yes!" from a positive place. And since this is your vision board—not your mother's, society's, your best friend's, your daughter's, or anyone else's who might want a say in how you go about your business— the only person who needs to feel like it appropriately reflects who they are and what they want is *you*. In that spirit, anything goes!

2. Placement. Arrange these images on a large piece of poster board or cardboard. The size is up to you, but I'd go with larger versus smaller. Then take the time to line up the cutouts in a way that feels right for you—emphasis on feeling. Notice how the words, images, and placement wake up your senses. Use your body and your brain to decide where they should ultimately go.

3. Commitment. Paste the words and images down onto the surface. Then look at your handiwork and decide if you feel it's reflective of a life and love that you want.

When you're done, consider what the board is telling you. Then name and claim what you want, and remain open to how it shows up in your life—because it may not come exactly as you imagined, says Cantwell. She recommends looking at your vision board frequently, at least three times a week, as a way to plant the information firmly into your subconscious and attract it to you.

"Creating a vision board is all about stimulating your brain," says Cantwell. "Priming yourself for what you want so when it comes to you, you can act on it."

Loving Hard, Being a Champion, and Calling the Shots

After going back and forth trying to decide if I could live with myself and Hector on his terms, I ultimately decided to let go, as you know. Knowing what I wanted and that I deserved it gave me the courage to put what I'd learned the hard way about love into play.

That started with my making a list that met all of my own criteria. And, after moving through Step Two, I was pretty sure of a few things:

1. I wanted to be happy, whether there was somebody special in my life or not.
2. I wanted to believe that my life was up to me.
3. I wanted to be with someone who wanted what I did and, as importantly, *when* I did. Because timing really can be everything.
4. I wanted to love consistently, without anger or fear or bitterness, no matter what or who was in my life.
5. I wanted to be with someone who was my spiritual, creative, and intellectual equal so they wouldn't be threatened or intimidated by my success or drive for it.
6. I wanted someone to be my champion, and I wanted to be a champion for them.
7. I wanted to learn and grow as a part of someone else's life, and have them learn and grow as part of mine.
8. I wanted someone who loved hard like I did. Who'd embrace the tidal wave of my love freely because I had a lot of it to give. And I was tired of holding back. A friend of mine once said she wanted someone who'd be in the "dance of love" with her for every step—no matter how fast, slow, easy, or difficult. I just adore that.

As I mentioned earlier, I wonder: If I'd been more fully grounded in knowing what I wanted earlier in my and Hector's relationship, would I have left sooner? With something more tangible like an end goal to shoot for, would I have been more hopeful and less reticent about taking the risk I needed to take to let go once and for all?

I'd like to think so. For me, and for you.

Knowing is powerful. Don't wait to figure it out. Instead, stake your claim. State it loudly and proudly. Make it your true north. And then let go for it, with the same focus and tenacity you gave to love that's failed you—that didn't deserve you (and you know what I'm talking about). Times two.

You just may be surprised by how it all turns out.

Although I won't be.

Chapter 7

THE OPTIONS

I was married, but it didn't work out, and so I left. My options for moving on were to first find the love I wanted with myself. Yes, I'll admit, I did go on the dating apps, but I recently deleted them. Even though I met some nice men, I realized that I needed to spend time getting to know myself first, before I could choose the right person. So, my options: To be on my own for a while. Travel with a friend to Europe, which we're planning. And put some perspective and fun back into my life and get happy. Then I'll be ready for what comes next.

—CeCe, 41, Brazil

When I was twenty-five years old, I was cleaning my studio apartment in Chicago on a Sunday afternoon when I got a phone call from a woman named Arlene. She owned a dating service in the suburbs and had picked my name out of a fishbowl at a Jewish art fair. She was calling to tell me I'd won the prize of a yearlong membership to her service. Was I interested?

I wasn't quite sure how to answer. After all, I'd never heard of her or that art fair—who even knew a Jewish art fair was a *thing*? And I certainly had no idea who'd entered me in that contest.

"Are you single?" she asked.

"Well, uh, sort of . . ." I don't know why I hesitated, since the answer was unabashedly yes.

"We've made a lot of matches, but if you're not interested, no problem," she said, sensing my hesitation. "I can pick another name."

Hold on now, I thought to myself. Did I really want to lose this opportunity? What if Arlene was the front woman for destiny? If I said no to her, would I live to regret it?

After all, the dating on my own wasn't going so well. Oh sure, I was out and about . . . but mostly with unavailable guys who'd behaved badly and were only moderately interested.

While I weighed the pros and the cons of Arlene's offer in my head, I scanned my apartment: I could practically shower, cook, sleep, and reorganize my closet all from the same spot in the living room.

Maybe it was time to broaden my horizons.

"Arlene," I said, "I'm in."

And off we went.

First I met with her assistant to go over my dating preferences and what I was looking for in a partner and a relationship. Then the fun began.

My first lunch date was twenty-one years old. Quiet and nervous, tall and skinny, with questionable skin and wearing a business suit three sizes too big, he was nowhere near the person I'd described to Arlene's assistant. But I made the best of it. After all, she and Arlene were experts. Maybe they knew something I didn't.

Over the next several months, I went on about eight dis-heartening dates. One of the more notable ones had me out with a full-on man of forty-three—a successful orthodontist who wore a lot of bracelets and was sort of cute for an old guy (back then, forty felt old).

It was the date I remember being the least horrid of them all, even though nothing came of it and he made me buy my own drink, which was not only sad, but also left me questioning Arlene's methods. How did she decide who to pair with whom? A roll of the dice? The tarot?

Because the twenty-one-year-old and the forty-three-year-old I met couldn't possibly be appropriate prospects for the same woman. To the contrary, the only thing they had in common was that they were both Jewish.

Wait a minute . . .

Mom.

Sure enough, she'd read about Arlene's dating service in the local Jewish newspaper in Philadelphia and signed me up. Told them to make up something plausible to get me in, knowing I'd never go for it if I knew she was behind it (I knew that Jewish art fair was suspect!). And while I appreciated my mother's "investment" in my finding a husband, I was mostly grateful for this lesson: that finding love on somebody else's terms was NOT an option.

At least not for me.

And yet . . .

While I wasn't on board with the reason behind Arlene's service (i.e., having somebody else find and assign me dates), it turned out that there was value in having ready access to other people like me, who were also seeking a partner. I might have rejected my mother's (boldly devious) efforts (I should have known she had it in her), but I had no idea back then that a more progressive version of Arlene's service—*online* dating—would become an option some seventeen years later, when I was newly single again after letting go of Hector.

What I liked about online dating was fairly obvious: it offered me more information (pictures!) about each prospect and the opportunity to pick and choose on my own terms. I was in control. I also believed that dating successfully was a numbers game, and online dating was a good way to increase my odds at winning—without having to rely on other people to fix me up, *or* hope that I would accidentally trip over a guy who was single, cute, ready for a commitment, and drawn to short, outgoing, curvy, red-headed Jewish girls.

What I didn't love about online dating was having to use technology to deal with matters of the heart; after all, there was enough new stuff to navigate just reacclimating to the opposite sex at that age. Fortunately, I had help. After divorcing my brother, my then sister-in-law had blazed that trail for herself, and she helped me set up a profile. She and my nieces also reminded me frequently, as I moved through the various stages of picking and meeting dates, that I was "the prize."

While I appreciated the cheering section, it also showed me how far I'd come since that early experience with Arlene and her service in both the dating and the self-love departments. I was no longer a deer in the headlights or willing to date somebody based on the sole criterion of their being interested.

I'd come to learn my worth and qualified my candidates accordingly, holding them up against who I was, what I wanted from love, and what I was willing to accept to get it. Knowing that happiness was an inside job, the stakes for finding someone felt much less dire than in the past. With my feet firmly planted in the deep soil of BWL, I moved gently into the experience and the next phase of my life.

Abundance Can Be Tricky

When it comes to choices, there's a lot at stake. Our lives call upon us daily to make one decision after the next—about where we live, the places we go, the things we do, the people we attach ourselves to, and so on. The hope is that we'll make good choices—and the ability to do so is one of the hallmarks of having a happy and fulfilling life.

And yet making choices can be tricky, especially if you lack Big Wild Love and allow limiting beliefs to guide you down the wrong paths. Here's another area where having large quantities of Big Wild Love works in your favor—by allowing you to make choices with consciousness and intention, the kind that lead you to the partner, relationship, and life that provide you with meaning.

With that in mind, you'll need this ground under your feet if you're looking for a way in or out of love at this particular moment in time, where the digital age has disrupted our dating culture to the point of excess. You'll need to use the BWL you've worked hard to cultivate to rise above the challenge of what to do when there are simply too many options, partners, and dating norms from which to choose.

It was a problem I didn't have way back when I was in my twenties because, good news or bad, there weren't a lot of options for folks looking to find love. There was no Internet, ergo no online dating; dating services were expensive and new and few and far between, and we generally met people in college or in bars or by some random freak accident.

Today, however, not only do people have options, but some might argue they have too many. Consider, for example, a study done at the University of Wisconsin-Madison, where researchers studied the glut of options on online dating sites and found that it didn't serve participants well.[24] They asked 152 undergrads to choose from a pool of potential dates. Some chose from a pool of twenty-four, while others chose from a pool of six. A week after making their selections, researchers found that those who chose from the larger group were less satisfied than those who chose from the smaller group—and more likely to change their mind. Those who'd chosen from the larger pool and had the subsequent option to pick a different person were the least satisfied with their choice of date after one week.

This is a problem that isn't likely to go away anytime soon. It's illustrative of the fact that while it's always good to have options, having too many can be counterproductive, leading to a perpetual sense of FOMO (Fear of Missing Out), regret, dissatisfaction, or worse.

Who would have ever thought that coming from a place of abundance in love and relationships would be troublesome? And yet it can be for folks who aren't grounded in who they are, what they want, and what they're willing to accept. Because without that, it's easy to get lost in so much choice.

Yet people are staying single longer than ever before, divorce is on the rise, and there is an unprecedented number of unmarried partners out there. According to the US Census Bureau, the median age for a first marriage is at its highest point since the census began—thirty years for men and twenty-eight years for women. And in 2015, for every one thousand married adults ages fifty and older, ten divorced—up from five in 1990. Among those age sixty-five and older, the divorce rate has roughly tripled since 1990.[25]

The divorce rate for those younger than fifty is about twice as high as it is for adults fifty and older. And since 1990, this rate has also climbed slightly for adults ages forty to forty-nine.

Given these odds, it would seem that your options for finding a suitable partner could be pretty good, as long as you remain focused on what you want and, just as importantly, how to go about getting it.

If you're single, you probably know by now that a popular option is the aforementioned dating online, as forty million Americans ranging from young to old are doing it, according to eharmony.com.[26] A 2016 report by the Pew Research Center shows that the number of eighteen- to twenty-four-year-olds dating online roughly tripled from 2013 to 2016, and that the rate of online dating participation has also risen significantly among fifty-five- to sixty-four-year-olds over the same period, from 6 percent to 12 percent.[27]

You need only log onto the growing list of dating sites and apps to see this phenomenon in action. It could literally take days to get through the streams of profiles available. I know because I did it. And I can tell you firsthand how difficult it is to move through them without a sense of confusion, doubt, and even paralysis. Whom should you choose? How can you trust what they say on their profile? After all, according to eharmony.com, 53 percent do lie. Maybe it's best to avoid it altogether. Be a spinster. The quirky and doting aunt who never married. And then there's the compulsion to never choose and, instead, bask in all that choice and live in hopeful denial . . . there's no pain or disappointment there. Just good coffee and Netflix.

Then there's what's happening offline: brick-and-mortar dating services that come with live human matchmakers like Arlene, fix-ups, bars, social media, Meetups, clubs for [insert hobby] enthusiasts, work, mastermind groups, classes, singles' nights and cruises and retreats and Outward Bounds and Inward Bounds and destination events—the list is endless.

Even if you're in a complicated relationship and not sure whether to hold on or let go, you have options: individual therapy, couples' therapy, sex therapy, couples' massage, yoga, medication, counseling, Club Med, websites that offer you discretionary infidelity, a weekend away in the Poconos, where heart-shaped beds and overflowing flutes of champagne promise to take you to an altered state. Nudist camps, wife-swapping, polyamory, separation, divorce, [insert ailment] Anonymous. The options can be mind-numbing.

It's like going to a New York City deli every day for the rest of your life. How many ways can you order your corned beef? (I've oddly thought a lot about this question.) In a Reuben, on a salad, as an entrée, on a regular sandwich, in an omelet, as hash, on a pizza, in a stromboli, etc. See where I'm going here?

What to do with so many ways to turn? If you haven't worked through your limiting beliefs, good luck. You may not agree with the statistics or the idea that there is actually someone out there for you and, instead, choose your sofa, a bottle of pinot grigio, and a weekend of karaoke on demand.

This is the story of Cathleen, a fifty-three-year-old librarian. After her divorce ten years ago, she decided that unless the right guy came knocking on her door, she was done. After all, she says, there's always a good book and Amazon Prime for a little fun. "While I'd love to find someone to spend the rest of my life with, I was also taught that I'm supposed to wait for a man to come to me, so I would never online date or even approach someone I liked first," she adds. "Besides, maybe that stuff is all behind me. I'm just fine at home by myself."

If you're in a relationship that's just not doing it for you, a combination of too much risk and too much choice may have you holding on to what you've got—flawed as it is—for dear life, instead of letting go for someone and something better.

Then there's working as many options as you can like a college senior at a job fair—fueled by both confidence and, yes, desperation. Like Pauline. A successful saleswoman who, divorced at forty-two, has left no stone unturned on her quest to find love. She online dates, offline dates, participates in Meetups, goes on singles cruises, blind dates, and anything else that increases her odds at coupledom. She's all over it.

She's also depleted, unfocused, and still single.

To which I asked her and Cathleen and, yes, you too: How's that working for you?

It was a question I also asked myself when I was that twenty-five-year-old girl, going to singles' nights at the grocery store across the street from my apartment (yep, a thing), asking friends to fix me up with mostly folks I had nothing in common with save for a pulse and a valid driver's license, even meeting prospects at the Department of Motor Vehicles (don't ask). I took all offers for dinner or coffee with few filters—it was the decade of yes, with limits when it came to sleeping together, of course. To the point of utter exhaustion.

Still, I thought the only way to meet someone was to keep moving. In looking back, I realize now that what I was really doing was letting an unchecked set of limiting beliefs and other people's voices in my head invite chaos into my love life: the kind of chaos that kept me sprinting, breathless, and pooped, but never getting anywhere.

Fortunately, I came to learn better, and so can you: that an unrelenting *lack* of focus may yield returns in the moment, but not the kind you're necessarily looking for or want.

And yet so many of us approach our options with this mindset. Instead of weighing the pros and cons of each option thoughtfully and moving forward accordingly, knowing we have the bandwidth for doing only so much, we rely on instinct, reflex, speed, fear, unchecked beliefs, and quantity over quality to drive our efforts.

We're taking my mother's approach by having no approach at all, "slapping enough shit up against the wall in the hopes that something will stick," as she likes to say. And while I love my mother, I find this method supremely misguided when it comes to identifying and exercising your options for finding a life partner. After all, what if what ultimately sticks is the human equivalent of old gum to your hair, or worse? Do you really want that?

And is it really about quantity of experiences versus quality? We may think that we'll make the best choices we can about our love life by having as many options as possible. But that's false. The way we ultimately make the best choices for ourselves is not based on the quantity of our options, but the quality.

Sure, love is a numbers game. I stand by that statement. But strategy is also required, especially if you're looking for healthy, happy, lasting love with a worthy, self-loving mate. In that case, I propose a route that's counter to my mother's idea of throwing excrement: one that doesn't require track shoes, a keg of Windex, a set of sturdy nose plugs, and disinfectant.

The Solution Is in the Planning

Here's the good news: now that you know what you want, you simply need to go through the exercise of what you need to do to get it. And there's lots of great stuff that can come from doing it. Having to negotiate a lot of options for how you'll find your way to your end goal drives not only a deeper clarity around that goal but also a commitment to achieving it.

This is, in fact, where the rubber hits the road—where the abstract becomes the tangible. Where identifying, choosing between, and executing on your options actually begins to yield rewards.

And while, as I stated in the previous section, working through your options can force you to a state of overwhelm, it can also force you to a state of intention. Which is precisely where you want to be: brimming with clarity and purpose.

If you've been doing the work I've asked of you up until this point—if you've been awake to your epiphany, present for your feelings, and clear on what you want next from love, a relationship, and even your life—you're ready to rumble.

Now's the time to lay out all roads that lead to your definition of home and then choose well between them. This moment is about focus, decision-making, and execution . . . figuring out the best way to get to your end goal with the least expenditure of time, effort, and resources.

It's about minimizing the steps to your destination.

When I was in graduate school, I waited tables at a very busy restaurant in the evenings and on weekends. I spent way too much time talking with my tables, delivering the wrong food to the wrong people, and trying to balance heavy trays of food with one hand while carrying the tray stand in the other, while a gaggle of busboys ran behind me, arms outstretched, sweating and cursing under their breath.

Yes, I was clumsy and chatty (two things I like to believe make me lovable), *but* I got the job done because I was efficient. I knew how to get all the tables in my section water, bread, extra butter, lunch, a bill, and the dessert menu in a series of condensed swoops. And as a result, people were not only forgiving of my shortcomings, but ate and left on a fairly swift rotation. In that sense, I knew what I was doing. My customers were happy they didn't have to wait. The restaurant was happy because I turned over my tables fast, generating more business. I had more money too. And I was rarely the last one left at the end of a shift, marrying the ketchup bottles and cashing out.

The point being this: identifying and executing your options is about minimizing your steps in terms of time, resources, and emotional expenditure. Because you're just one person. And it's likely you have a job, friends, family, and a life that also need tending. You don't have all the time and focus in the world to wade through the myriad of options available to you for finding love, and you don't need to go on a hundred Internet dates to find your guy or gal—unless you want to, don't know what you want, or are not big wild loving enough to set the appropriate criteria and boundaries.

You just need to keep being strategic.

You know the "what." Now it's time to figure out the quickest, easiest, most painless way to "how."

And to make peace with the idea that getting where you want to go will be a process.

For Janice, the forty-three-year-old writer you met in chapter 4, she knew that, after she'd left her husband Collin, she wanted to be with Joe, now her husband. But she needed to thoughtfully lay out her options for getting there.

"I knew I needed a job first, and began working on that so I could live on my own," she says. "Because I didn't always know that Joe was an option for sure and didn't want to move in with him right away. I needed time out of my marriage to really explore that. I also had to figure out the options for doing so, for bringing our kids together peacefully and in a way that was good for everybody, for finding our way to the life we both wanted. Whenever we felt lost or confused, we'd go back to that. It allowed us to stay focused and create a plan that worked. But we needed a plan for sure."

It took time to get where she and Joe wanted to go, as all good things do. But it eventually all fell into place. She had options and a plan. And you will too. If you continue to love yourself like peanut butter loves jelly, Ben loves Jerry, and I love black yoga pants, I have no doubt that you'll be able to craft a set of options that will get you precisely where you want to go, which is [insert here].

Just checking.

Whittling Your Options Down to Three

OK, so let's do this.

If there are fifteen ways for you to logically and perhaps logistically find love, you don't need to attempt them all at once. In fact, as you may have surmised by now, I don't recommend it. Instead, get pointed. In this section, we're going to chip away at those options together so you're left with a very reasonable plan for execution.

There is a method to my madness of wanting you to pare your options down, one based in science. One study after another confirms that when it comes to making choices, keeping your options to a minimum is the best, most fruitful, and most manageable way to go.

An article in the *Harvard Business Review* lays out the hypothesis that if you think more is better when it comes to choosing from a set of options, you're wrong.[28] In the study featured in the article, psychologists from Columbia and Stanford Universities set up a tasting booth at an upscale grocery store in California. On some days, they put out a selection of six types of jam; on other days, they set out twenty-four. They found that although a wider selection attracted more shoppers, more people bought the jam when there were fewer options. It seemed the more choices people had, the harder it was to make a decision.

This is aligned with the research I referred to earlier and other studies on the subject. It also forms the basis of my recommended approach and the work that follows: less is more.

With that in mind, the following exercises are designed to help you first pull back to the big picture and then whittle your options down from there. Grab your journal and let's get to work.

Step #1

Write down what you want, as a result of the work done in the previous chapter. Create a main objective and then lay out what you want under it across four main components; be specific.

Main objective: What's the real, real, real end goal? Big pic?

1. What you want in a partner. Not in terms of physical attributes, but deeper—from a values, morals, interests, personality, and integrity perspective.
2. What you want from a relationship. Do you want to get married, live with someone, just be monogamous, have an open relationship?
3. What you want for your life, logistically. Do you want to live in one specific area, be open to travel, see the world?
4. Deal breakers and red flags. Because you'll need to keep this in front of you once you've laid out your options and you're ready to see them through.
5. How you would like to feel in the relationship.

Given these categories, your entry may look something like this:

Main objective: To find someone to be in a happy and healthy, long-term, no drama relationship with (another objective could be about finding self-love through the process of realigning your beliefs, or letting go of a particular issue that you can't seem to get past inside of an otherwise good relationship).

1. *What you want in a partner.*

a. BIG WILD LOVING, LIKE YOU.

b. Someone who has kids since you do too.

c. Someone who's business-minded, since you're creative and would like that for balance.

d. Someone who's into sports and physical fitness.

e. Someone who's been married before, understands the commitment involved, and wants to get married again.

f. Someone who has a lot of sisters and understands and appreciates women.

g. Someone who is independent and is OK with spending time alone.

2. *What you want from a relationship.*

a. Marriage

3. *What you want for your life (logistically).*

a. To live in Austin, Texas, because that's where your family, friends, and job are.

4. *Deal breakers and red flags regarding a prospective partner:*

a. Clueless about their beliefs on love and their worth.

b. Single and forty and living at home.

c. Living in another state and not wanting to move.

d. Never been married.

e. Been married more than three times.

f. Confused about the future.

g. Wants to date around.

h. Likes okra and punk rock.

i. Looking for a texting buddy but doesn't want to meet.

j. Doesn't like to make plans for dinner or the future.

k. Has hard and fast rules about life and makes lots of generalizations about things.

l. Is hardheaded.

m. Is a narcissist.

n. Enjoys picking his nose in public.

o. Vehemently disagrees with my politics.

p. Lacks deep, meaningful friendships.

q. (You get it . . .)

5. *How you'd like to feel in the relationship.*

a. Loved, secure, confident, helpful, seen, valued

Step #2

Hold the deal breakers and red flags for now. Put the first three items into a chart and add a column for your "options." In that column, you're going to put down all the many things you can do to get to each "want." For example:

To find someone to be in a happy and healthy, long-term, no drama relationship with . . .		
	What I want . . .	**How I get it . . .**
Partner	Has boatloads of BWL, likes/has kids, business-minded, into sports and physical fitness, married before, understands and appreciates women, independent, etc.	Fix-ups from friends who get it, dating online, dating services, singles' events, Meetup groups, athletic groups and events, place of worship, cooking classes or book readings that feature female authors, business seminars or workshops, playgrounds and playdates with kids, school events
Relationship	Marriage	Support groups for divorce or widowhood (if appropriate), fix-ups, dating online, dating services, singles' events, Meetup groups, athletic groups, religious groups, etc.
Life	Live in Texas	Community-based religious, political, hobby and volunteer organizations, local friends, work, etc.

Take as much time as you need with this chart and put in as many options as you can possibly think of, including those that are local and specific to who you are and what you want. The more specific, the better. Be sure to include a variety of options that involve all types of environments—online, offline, face-to-face, etc. Ask your friends for their thoughts. Do some research on what's available to you in the community so you can be specific about where you can go and what clubs you can join to meet people, especially if you're looking to put down roots in that community. Or, if you're looking to build a life someplace other than where you are (you want to go there for a job, friends, the climate, etc.), investigate what's happening in your desired locale.

If you get stuck, do some free-form journaling around the question, "Given what I want, what are the different ways I can get it?" And then go back to the chart and keep writing until you've exhausted every option and idea.

Step #3

This is where you'll curate your options, distilling them down to three doable tactics that—executed well, with commitment and diligence—can get you where you want to go. Before we get started, consider a study published in the journal *Organizational Behavior and Human Decision Processes* that had researchers from business schools in the UK and Singapore examine how two different ways of evaluating options can influence people's choices. Across seven experiments, 2,783 participants were asked to make choices from options that were presented either sequentially or all at once. Some decisions were simple, such as which camera model to buy; others were more complex, such as which supplier to award a contract to. Overall, the results show that people were, on average, 22 percent more likely to choose the objectively best option when they viewed options together rather than one at a time.[29]

With the results of this study in mind, I'm going to ask you to review all of your options in one place, rather than segregating them and evaluating them that way. (In fact, if online dating is one of your options, this is precisely how you're going to review people's profiles as well—by paring them down. Putting them onto a page together, even if you have to print each of their pages out separately and then literally cut and paste images onto a separate page.)

Look at the chart you created in the previous exercise and pull out all the options you've listed in the right column onto a

separate page so you can see them all together. Put stars next to
those options you've mentioned several times or across each row.

As you move through this exercise, keep a few last caveats
in mind:

- Don't discount online dating simply because you may find
  it overwhelming; it is a viable option for finding love and
  winning the game of numbers involved. Instead, be targeted about your search. Keep your list of deal breakers
  and red flags taped to the computer and close, so you can
  see them as you browse profiles. Then choose no more
  than six profiles or six people with whom you've had at
  least one back-and-forth exchange. Lay each of their pictures or anything else you'd like to compare out on a page
  and choose three of the six to reach out to.

- Make sure whatever options you choose are realistic and
  doable in the context of your life (e.g., time, obligations,
  commitments, resources, etc.). And, not least importantly,
  have fun! This is dating, not a colonoscopy.

- Be aware of any limiting beliefs that come up as you move
  through this process and quickly address and reframe
  them. If you must, go back to chapter 3 for a refresher on
  how to do this.

- As you begin to meet people and even get involved in a
  relationship (or engage in a current relationship with new
  parameters), remember how you want a relationship to
  make you feel. If you're not feeling those things given the
  appropriate amount of time (for example, you may not
  feel loved or secure after just one date), it may be time to
  reassess whether that situation is right for you and how
  or if you can create change.

Step #4

Based on the three options you select, create a list of three action steps for each as a way to get them underway. Track your progress in your journal or on a calendar, whatever works best for you. Either is fine, as long as you keep your end goal and action steps front and center so you actually do them.

My Three Options Did the Trick and Then Some

Yes, I went through this exercise myself and found it extremely helpful. It forced me to wade through my cluttered and tired mind and fearful albeit hopeful soul, once I'd let go of Hector. At the end of the day, my three options involved:

1. Leaving Chicago and moving to New Hope, Pennsylvania.
2. Getting out into the community once I'd arrived to meet people by taking a part-time job at a boutique, making unattached friends, and frequenting a local restaurant on the weekends where I knew like-minded singles gathered.
3. Online dating.

Knowing I ultimately wanted to make my way back home, closer to the area where I'd grown up, family, and childhood friends, I decided moving back to New Hope, a small artists' community in between Philadelphia and New York, was a great option.

Knowing that I wanted a relationship that would go the distance, that I wanted marriage and commitment with someone who had all the things I mentioned in the previous chapter, I was determined that I could get to it a few ways: first, by putting myself out into the community, making new friends who could introduce me to new prospects, and meeting local singles where they were.

I also saw the promise of online dating almost immediately, once I'd overcome my fear of technology and let go of a few other limiting beliefs that had newly surfaced (I'll talk more about that in the next chapter).

What was notably different in my approach to finding love this time was the mindset of wanting to enjoy life. I embraced my new life and status as a single woman with a sense of fun and play, squelching limiting beliefs when they tried to resurrect themselves in my brain, and holding onto perspective. Remembering that, as challenging and new as it was, online dating, or any of it for that matter, wasn't a matter of life and death. Getting "results" didn't feel as dire as it did when I was younger. The pressures of convention didn't weigh on me as heavily as they once had.

By that point, I was mostly interested in being happy and peaceful and content, and I was perfectly fine with honing and refining my definition of what each of those things meant. The desperation I'd once felt around meeting someone no longer had the same vise grip on me as it had when Arlene called me on that fateful Sunday. If I met someone to share my life with, great, but if I didn't, well, that was OK, too, as I've said over and over in these pages.

I meant it.

After all, I'd already found my way to the love story I wanted most.

Knowing that gave me the strength, courage, joy, and fortitude I needed to venture out into the unknown worlds of online and offline dating.

I highly recommend it.

Chapter 8

THE LETTING GO HIT LIST

My super "let it go" moment was leaving my husband and then letting go of being terrified of being lonely, because I was already lonely in my marriage. Then I tried online dating and had to let that go, too, because I needed to spend time with myself. Now I'm running a half marathon and planning travel with a friend. It's good. While I don't know if I'll ever meet anyone else or even have sex again (you can laugh at this one), I'm letting go of those things too. Along with the fact that I have no control over other people. I know now that no matter what happens and when, I'll be fine.

—Priscilla, 40, Montana

And so it began: my journey into the world of online dating. There were so many sites to navigate—Match.com, Yahoo. com, JDate, and eHarmony, to name just a few—where would I begin? How could I attract the right kinds of guys? What should I say in my profile?

I was a fish out of water, eager, yes, but confused and over-whelmed by this new way of prospecting for love. I needed a way in—a winning strategy. After all, I was determined to let Big Wild Love guide me this time around.

With my list of deal breakers and my end goal taped securely to the top of my computer, I was ready to go, but I was also scared. I was venturing into the potentially light—and dark—unknown. What if I wrote to people and they didn't write back? If the only people who wrote to me were those I had no interest in? If I went on a date with the wrong person and wound up in some dumpster (note to self: less Lifetime television)? If I couldn't trust myself to make good choices after all? If nobody wanted me? If the limit-ing beliefs I'd worked so hard to get rid of were right and I was destined to be alone forever?

It was clear that I needed to find a way to take the charge out of the experience as I got closer to going through with it. So I decided to approach it as if I were a reporter writing an arti-cle for *Jill Can Find Healthy Love After 40*, a fictitious magazine named for my newly empowered belief system. After all, I'd been a journalist for decades. Surely using this as a device would help me get going.

To cover the story from all angles, I registered on as many dating sites as was reasonable, including the four mentioned above. I also considered the sage advice of friends who'd blazed the trail before me: Don't go out with guys who don't post a picture or who've never been married, since they're probably commitment-phobic. Don't engage with someone who wants to e-mail but never meet, because they're probably married or worse. Don't talk to someone for too long before actually seeing them in person, so you don't get too invested too fast and then find out there's no physical attraction.

I took detailed notes, inhaled deeply, and then tossed myself into cyberspace like someone jumping out of an airplane. It was a rite-of-passage leap of faith, this idea I could meet someone meaningful through the vehicle of an algorithm and a graphic user interface. The good news was that it didn't take long for me to get the hang of it. Within days, I was scrolling through profiles with glee, exchanging e-mails with prospects like trading cards. I'm not saying they were all good prospects—or that eHarmony didn't match me with five unusually short men and a woman named Elizabeth—because they did and that was weird. Instead of getting hung up about how that happened, I stayed focused on my end goal and very active queue of prospects.

After about three weeks, I found myself going on my first real live date with a guy named Andrew whom, I'll admit, I'd probably spent too much time e-mailing and talking to on the phone before meeting. I say that because the date, at least for me, did not go well. We met at a restaurant for dinner. Not only did he look twenty pounds heavier and twenty years older than his picture, he also used his hands to eat off of my plate without asking, licked his fingers, talked with food in his mouth, didn't have much of a sense of humor in person, and couldn't wait to introduce me to his mother. He was considerably different than the person I'd come to know online and by telephone.

Suffice it to say, it was an eight-thousand-hour date (or so it felt) that ended on the bridge between New Hope and Lambertville. Nobody jumped, although I'd be lying if I said I hadn't contemplated it as a way to excuse myself. He simply went in for a romantic moment and I responded by coughing . . . a lot. And yes, I'm sure there was a more delicate way to handle that, but I did send him a kind "thanks but no thanks" note after the fact.

I had more luck on the next go around with Mack. Good

looking, charismatic, fun, kind, and successful, he had me at hello. The problem was we'd have a great time together and then he'd disappear for weeks at a stretch, eventually breaching the silence with a same-day invitation for dinner.

To which I said yes, three times. Until I recognized the old Jill resurfacing, falling back into familiar self-sabotaging habits. The old me would've seen Mack's unreliability as an opportunity to either fix him or win him over. She would have taken his ghosting personally, read it as evidence of her being defective in some way that she needed to overcome. She would have ridden shotgun on the road to nowhere for as long as he'd have let her. Three dates would have led to three years . . . or longer.

But this new me knew better and decided there would be no fourth date. That I just needed to keep trucking.

That was a big day for BWL.

Then there was the guy who e-mailed me a love poem he said he'd "written" just for me, which turned out to be plagiarized lyrics to a Depeche Mode song.

Some other notables:

The neurolinguistics programmer who suggested I drive ninety minutes to his house and sleep with him to see if we were a match, before he spent money on a real date.

The guy who told me I looked thinner in my pictures and should lose some weight.

The other one who told me his sole goal in life was to make his ex-wife miserable.

Yup, it was an adventure, all right. And I learned a few things along the way: while I was making progress in the self-love department, I still had work to do around letting go.

Lingering beliefs I thought I'd long released had begun to reappear, like the idea that I had to be a perfect size six to be loved. That

I should take only what I could get. I had also acquired some new fears about love and life and aging that I needed to keep in check.

Fortunately, I now knew how to do that. I also knew that when life offered up the challenges of change, it also offered new opportunities for self-exploration and understanding, and letting go as a result.

And if I was smart, I'd take them.

Keeping Your Eyes Open for Deer . . . and *Letgoables*

When I first embarked on my journey of letting go, I was sure that once I'd let go of Hector and my life in Chicago, I'd be ready to rule the world. That was it: one and done. I'd wiped the Etch A Sketch clean and I was ready to start anew. Yay for me.

And then, reality . . .

I have to laugh at how naïve I was, thinking that the act of letting go was a one-and-done deal. That just letting go of Hector along with my life in Chicago would be enough to get me where I ultimately wanted to go.

It wasn't. Not by a long shot.

The truth is, while I'd found tremendous clarity through letting go of Hector as well as my beloved Chicago, it was just the start. Each new step into each new experience thereafter required me not only to get comfortable with discomfort, but also to loosen my grip and love myself a little harder. Nowhere was that truer than in navigating the world of online dating, which taught me that when it came to my pursuit of Big Wild Love, my work wasn't done.

I also learned that it never would be. That as long as I left the comfort and safety of my house, attempted anything new in life, initiated change, or found myself on the receiving end of what I didn't want, I'd need an ongoing relationship with letting go in order to sustain the life and love I wanted most.

I'd need to use the act of letting go as both a practice and a tool I could reach for whenever I needed to get out of my own way.

And so, too, do you.

Part of doing this successfully hinges on knowing when it's time to let go: the answer is when something just feels *off*. When your otherwise healthy body tingles in a way that compels you to attention. When you find yourself struggling over and over again in love and relationships (and frankly, anywhere else), never getting any further along or closer to what you want.

These are all clear signs that there are still what I call "letgoables" on the table, and they need to be addressed. And yes, I made that word up for clarity and ease of use—a letgoable being anything you need to let go of, pure and simple. That can include people, situations, beliefs, thoughts, ideas, voices, and anything else you're holding on to that keeps you standing in your own way.

Letgoables can travel alone, but they usually don't. It's more often the case that when you have one letgoable, there are several more just waiting to be called out. And if you don't acknowledge and address each and every one of them—sometimes all at once—you might very well wind up shortchanging your efforts and your results.

Because we can't just let go of a relationship or a person and think we're ready to do better the next time. There is a holistic component to letting go that is critically necessary in making sure you get to your end goal—one that requires you to peel back the layers of your external and internal realities at the very same time to understand what you're holding on to, what's serving, and what isn't.

Unfortunately, very few people, after leaving a partner or situation, or trying to survive inside of one, actually do this. They fail to address the full set of letgoables in a way that sets them up for success on the next go-around. They don't stop to ask, What else do I need to let go of, besides the person or the partnership in part or whole, to get what I want?

This was certainly true for Lissa, the thirty-year-old accountant I introduced in chapter 4. When I interviewed her, I asked her what she felt she needed to let go of beyond her last boyfriend and relationship in order to find the healthy, happy love she wanted. In response, she rattled off a list of letgoables that surprised even herself.

"Well, I mostly need to let go of finding a guy who's masculine, successful, and a provider, like my father, because I'm not sure he even exists," she says, adding that even though she can take care of herself, she always saw her income as being supplemental to her partner's in a relationship.

Then, upon further thought, she said this: "I guess I also need to let go of being so judgmental about guys who not only make less than me, but where and how I meet them. For example, if I meet them in a bar, I think less of them than if I meet them at a business event or even the gym. I discount them almost immediately. But why? I'm at the bar, too, and I don't judge myself in the same superficial way. It makes me sad to think about how many guys I've cast aside before really getting to know them and giving them a chance to know me."

Lissa kept drilling down on her letgoables during the course of our conversation, realizing that she makes it hard for most guys to both approach and get to know her because she's afraid they'll eventually see the real her behind the confident veneer she projects. They'll see "the imposter," she says, "the scariest parts of me that aren't perfect, light, or free, like I feel love and relationships should be."

And then, the biggest letgoable of them all: the fear of being hurt.

"I've been so deeply impacted by the people I've let in and who've left me that I haven't yet decided whether it's worth giving someone else years of my life, only to wind up destroyed. I probably also need to stop projecting my heaviness around relationships onto others . . . or thinking I should always say 'no' first instead of why I should say 'yes.'"

"Goodness," she said, taking in these revelations. "It's so exhausting, carrying all of this stuff . . ."

Yes, it is.

And wow. Just wow.

It was clear to me during our exchange that this was the very first time Lissa had actually gone through such an exercise. And she's not alone.

So many people have no idea what's lurking under the surface, including many of the women I spoke to, who'd not only struggled to let go of their partners and relationships, but had little residual bandwidth for treasure hunting for more things to let go of (and trust me, there is treasure).

They were tired and unsure, and the last thing they wanted was to dig deeper inside to do more work. They figured they'd cracked the big nut; anything else could either wait or wouldn't hurt them.

But it not only hurt them, they kept falling into the same old traps that prevented them from attracting suitable partners, maintaining suitable relationships, and even moving smoothly and productively past heartbreak.

It's like seeing a deer in the road while driving. You know when one deer races out in front of you that there are likely several more right behind it, ready to get you into trouble. That's your sign: to slow down, look around, take stock. Ignore that first deer, and you've got problems. Ignore the others, and you've still got problems. To get to your destination safely, you've got to see them all.

Letting go works the same way. It's not a one-and-done deal. You've got to do it in bulk.

Here's an example of what I'm talking about: you can't let go of a relationship and expect to find a new, healthier one without letting go of the limiting beliefs that got you where you didn't want to go originally. And if you've got a lot of anxiety or fear about going inside of yourself to uncover those limiting beliefs, you'll need to let go of that emotion and subjectivity so you can be productively objective and introspective. And if you can't let go of the opinions of other people who may have given you those limiting beliefs in the first place, you won't get too far. So you'll need to let go of their voices in your head as well, making sure yours always rises to the top. And if you have trouble doing that and need help, but don't believe that seeking support is appropriate, you'll need to let go of that little darling as well . . .

See where I'm going?

There are all kinds of ways that holding on to what seems like the most innocuous of things can keep you from making progress. Letting go comprehensively, through awareness, allows you to move things along at a more desirable clip. And yes, it also requires you to multitask, walk and chew gum at the same time, so you can negotiate more than one issue at a time. And yes, we're not necessarily great at that, as researchers at Stanford University found that regular multitasking makes it harder for people to prioritize and focus.[30] Which is why letting go on this scale can be challenging, and we need to be especially vigilant as we do it. Still, we must do it.

It was only when I'd come to understand that letting go of Hector was just the beginning—that I had to also let go of the life I'd built around him, the regret I'd felt in overstaying my welcome, and the voices telling me I had to be perfect to be loved, I'd be crazy to leave after investing so much time, or that starting over with someone new was a pipe dream—that I began to make headway.

Letting go comprehensively was painful, that's the truth. But it was also what saved me.

What allowed me to be brave and bold as I moved through the process of dating, online and otherwise.

What gave me the courage to post a profile on one website, let alone four.

What gave me the wherewithal to walk away from Mack, who was adorable, charming, sexy, funny, and unavailable (sound familiar?), whom I really, really, really, really, really, really liked, and who pulled all of my old triggers, as evidenced by how quickly I found myself wrapped up in what he needed more than in what I did. Just three dates in—a sure sign that I still had letgoables to contend with.

Which brings me to this: when it comes to letting go, there's more than just a partner or a relationship to consider. That's a great beginning, but you need to keep going. Ongoing self-exploration is where the rubber hits the road. It will allow you to uncover hidden saboteurs—thoughts, ideas, beliefs, situations, other people, relationships and even friendships, other people's voices or judgment, the pressures of culture, convention, regret, whatever—that will keep you stuck if you let them. Instead, let them go too. And then stay attentive. Keep your eyes wide open on that open highway of relationship. Use the act of letting go as a practice.

The good news is that when you do, you get to reclaim old and new parts of yourself that ultimately move you closer to your end goal.

Which begs the question: What *else* do you need to let go of?

The Five Agreements and Then Some

I don't know if you've noticed, but we're having a letting go movement. The Japanese decluttering specialist Marie Kondo has elevated the concept of letting go to levels so high, we're now using her name as an actual verb. I'm sure you'd all agree there's a great sense of accomplishment that comes with purging the stuff we no longer need or want. After all, when we lighten our load and get rid of what's no longer working, we open up space for what does. When we prune out the junk in our closets, we can actually see what we've got and go productively from there.

All of this seems fairly simple when it comes to cleaning out the junk drawer in the kitchen. But when it comes to letting go of people, relationships, and even intangible letgoables like beliefs, feelings, thoughts, and ideas, it's hard to know where to even begin.

In this section, I'm going to give you some ideas so you can create a letting go "hit list" that you can then work from to purge the letgoables standing between you and what you want.

There are lots of things you can let go of that you may, or may not, be aware of. For now, just know that your list is likely longer than you think. And that as your awareness of it grows and you begin to release stuff, you might feel like your possibilities for love will get smaller.

To the contrary, they'll be better possibilities. Moving down your letting go hit list will allow you to prune the weeds so you can finally see where the flowers are. And, as importantly, where it will be worth your while to spend time tending the soil.

Because here's what happens as your Big Wild Love increases, which hopefully it has as you've moved through the pages of this book: you will find that your tolerance for people who no longer meet you where you are will decrease. As a result, so too will the number of people you'll be willing to either date or engage with in a relationship. And that's not only OK, it's great, because you'll be raising the bar and using a higher quality set of criteria to make choices about whom you give your time to. Creating a letting go hit list will help you not only whittle down but also better qualify the playing field so you can be more discerning and focus less on tending to *all* of the possibilities, and more on the probabilities. So you can actually get somewhere . . .

In my TEDx talk, I offer five letgoables as a way to get started. One of my viewers actually called them the "five agreements," as a nod, I suspect, to Don Miguel Ruiz's *The Four Agreements*—a book I keep on my coffee table and often give as a gift. If you've never read it, I strongly encourage you to do so, as it's both poetic and full of practical wisdom.

While I believe the five agreements are essential for getting to healthy and happy love, you might be interested to know there were other letgoables I wanted to share in my talk but couldn't due to time constraints. Which is why I'm delighted to share them with you here. As you review, consider how you might incorporate them into your own journey.

Nine Letgoables for a Happy Life and Relationship

1. **Let go of taking things personally:** Especially other people's bad behavior, because that has nothing to do with you and everything to do with them. Again, we are mirrors for other people, always reminding them of what they are and what they aren't. We can't control how they respond to us or whether they've done their own work cultivating BWL, but we can choose to disassociate ourselves from their actions, words, and behaviors so we don't get distracted from our own goals.

2. **Let go of what other people think:** Not everybody is going to like you, agree with you, support you, want to be with you, etc. Learn to be OK with that. Because what they think of you or want for you doesn't matter. As long as you're not intentionally hurting someone else, it's your life to do with as you please. At fifty-six, I'm finally coming to understand this fully myself and it's utterly freeing. I only wish I'd gotten it sooner!

3. **Let go of being something you're not:** Because who you are is awesome! You're one of a kind, so flaunt it. Besides, it's impossible to be something or someone else. Oh sure, you might be able to keep up the façade for a while. But one good stomach flu, sleepless night, or disappointing e-mail from the IRS, and the real you is bound to emerge.

4. **Let go of the need to be perfect:** You've got a 100 percent failure rate here. Instead, just do your best. And remember that perfection is not only impossible, it's also overrated. After all, would you want to be friends with someone who was perfect? Nah, me neither.

5. **Let go of the need for closure:** Even if the guy or gal who dumped you or cheated on you sat you down and gave you a bullet-point list of why they behaved as they did, would you believe them? The truth is you may never know why people do what they do. And unless you're trying to solve a bona fide crime, find the space in your mind for it to no longer matter. Instead, rely on yourself for the closure you need to keep moving forward.

6. **Let go of unproductive fear:** We need some fear to keep us safe in the face of life-threatening danger, but we don't need the kind of fear that keeps us stuck in non-life-threatening situations that aren't serving us well. Like, for example, the fear that if we leave our dissatisfying relationship, we'll be doomed. Or that if we're over age forty, our best years are behind us. The good news is that according to the National Institute of Mental Health, 90 percent of what you fear is insignificant, and 60 percent will never take place anyway.

7. **Let go of regret:** So, I never got to be on the Oprah show, looking fabulous in a sequined catsuit, promoting my best-selling memoir and naming all the men who'd wronged me while they each sat in the front row, crying and mouthing the words "I'm sorry." That's OK. I also didn't have children. Didn't become a reporter for *Rolling Stone* magazine. Never had a townhouse in Manhattan. Or worked stages as a concert pianist. None of that happened. But so many other wonderful things did! And that's where I put my focus. Wouldn't it be great if we all had flux capacitors to transport us back in time so we could do a few things over? Sadly, that only happens in the *Back to the Future* movies. Barring that, regret is

a waste of precious time. Instead, focus on gratitude for all you have and all that is ahead of you.

8. **Let go of doing other people's work:** This one really gets my goat. I can't tell you how many women I've coached who've spent hours pontificating on what their significant others said or didn't say or do, and why. *"But then he said this . . . did this . . . he's scared . . . I think he just doesn't remember or is too worried about or . . . "* Blah, blah, blah (sorry). Any time you find yourself starting a sentence with any of the above italicized phrases, stop talking and redirect (I think you'll be shocked by how often you need to do this). Start the next sentence with "I feel, I am, I want . . . " Stay focused on *your* motivation and not the other person's. That's what really matters.

9. **Let go of not yet:** What are you waiting for? Take the risk. Love yourself. Leap. After all, we only have this moment. What are you going to do with it?

Create Your Own Letting Go Hit List

OK, now it's your turn. Crack open your journal. It's time to start listing out what you need to let go of.

Step #1

Make that list. If you're not sure or you're stuck, feel free to reach into the nine letgoables I laid out in the previous section as prompts. There's also a longer list at the end of this section, so you can either pull from there as well or use some of what's on that list as an example for you to build on. Either way, be comprehensive and don't censor yourself. Whatever you think will point you toward having the life and love you want, add it to the list. There are no right or wrong answers. Everything is fair game.

Step #2

Once you've created your list, circle three items you think are the easiest to achieve—the low-hanging fruit, if you will—and put them through the following exercise, so you can take action on them and enjoy some quick wins. Then keep going by choosing three more. I encourage you to make this next go-around about selecting letgoables that may not be as easy, but once reframed could lead to the biggest breakthroughs of them all.

As you continue putting them and other letgoables through the following paces, you'll soon see a pattern emerge that will give you important insights about what's holding you back and where you need to make improvements in your own BWL, all of which will be super big for you and your results.

Step #3

For each item that's circled, answer the following questions.
- Write down the letgoable.
- What is the limiting belief attached to it? If you need to refresh yourself on what a limiting belief is, go back to chapter 2. It's important to identify the limiting belief that's attached to the letgoable so that you can address it.
- Rewrite the belief in an empowering way. Reframe it and your thinking so the limiting belief is either gone and/or newly working in your favor.
- Write a paragraph that shows how the empowering belief will play out in practice. This is all about rewriting the story you tell yourself. The old limiting belief will have shaped the narrative in a way that prevents you from

reaching your end goal. Let the new, more positive belief shape it in a way that lifts you closer toward it.

- Provide the evidence for this new story. I'm talking about the black-and-white, indisputable facts that shape the case for your new empowering belief and the story associated with it. This can include statistics, other people's success stories, irrefutable truths and observations, historical events or activities, etc. It can even include BWL (e.g., the proof that the new story is possible is that you have *you*, and you're smart and determined and worthy).

The reason I want you to spend time on this is that it's easy for us to get lost in our heads . . . to believe that, despite factual and objective proof that the sky is blue, the sky is actually bright orange, because that's what we've been conditioned to believe for so many years by the people and/or experiences that have had the greatest influence on us.

Here are a few examples of how the answers to these questions could look:

Example #1:
- What was the letgoable? Let go of thinking I'm too fat to be loved.
- What was the limiting belief attached to it? I need to have a perfect body to be loved by another person.
- What was the new empowering version? I am beautiful and lovable and have a lot to offer the right person, who will appreciate all I bring to his/her life.
- What was the new one-paragraph story? I am excited about what lies ahead. I am a beautiful and curvaceous woman who enjoys being in a relationship with someone

who values all that I bring to the table. I know he/she is out there, just ready to enjoy life and love with me because I am enjoying life on my own and love myself enough to know what I'm worth. I have never struggled to find someone to go out with in the past, but now I'm looking to take those choices to a whole new level. I'm looking for something and someone different—someone who is as evolved as I am when it comes to knowing what counts most. A person and a relationship that celebrates my femininity and all that I am. I know that going forward, this attitude will attract the right person to me. Someone who will share my values, interests, and hobbies, who will appreciate my aesthetic, and who will share my long-term goal to be in a healthy, happy relationship.

- What was the evidence?
  - I have always been able to attract members of the opposite sex, no matter what my size or what the scale says.
  - I have had happy and successful relationships with friends and family and outside of romantic love that prove that the size of my body is irrelevant to whether I'm worthy.
  - I just ran a 5K and did really well, so clearly my body is strong and serving me in a good way.
  - My body is healthy and strong and allows me to enjoy an active and productive quality of life . . . I am perfect just as a I am.

Example #2:
- What was the letgoable? Let go of believing nobody will want me because I'm over forty.
- What was the limiting belief? I'm too old to find love.

- What was the new empowering version? I am in the prime of my life and have a lot of experience, wisdom, and maturity to offer to the right person who wants what I do and who I know is out there waiting for me, when I'm ready.

- What was the new story? I believe that life begins at forty. I wouldn't want to go backward. I now know what's important and what isn't. Especially when it comes to relationships, because I've been there. Made my mistakes and learned from them. As a result, I know precisely what I'm looking for, what I'm willing to accept and what I'm not. I have no regrets. I'm also no longer afraid to be alone because I love myself and being with myself. And I know that no matter what happens, my life will be good and happy because I'll make it such, no matter who comes into my life. The fact is I'm delighted that my life experiences have led me to being the person I am today, and I know that whoever comes into my life next will feel the same way because I will accept nothing less. I'm driving the bus now. He/she will value the experience, wisdom, and maturity I bring to our relationship and will offer me the same.

- What was the evidence?
  - Statistics that show how people are finding love again after forty.
  - Statistics that show divorce is on the rise, which means there are more prospects in the dating pool after a certain age.
  - A list of the cadre of new dating websites targeted to people of a certain age, proof that there's a market. After all, nobody starts a business if they don't think they have a viable audience for what they're offering.

○ I've had friends and family members who've divorced or lost partners and gone on to find love again with a healthy, happy partner—point to success stories you've witnessed.

One Hundred Potential Letgoables

1. A bad relationship
2. A bad partner
3. A toxic friendship
4. A toxic family member
5. The feeling of being stuck
6. The feeling of being jealous
7. The feeling of hurt from a former cheating spouse or partner
8. The feeling of betrayal
9. Fear of living alone forever
10. Anger toward another person
11. The idea that it's all on me to make love work
12. The idea that it's all on me to make another person happy
13. The idea that I'm not good enough to be loved
14. The idea that no one will ever love me
15. The feeling of watching a parent stay in an abusive relationship
16. The feeling of watching a parent be abused or an abuser
17. The idea that I don't have a right to ask for what I want
18. The idea that in asking for what I want, I'm being selfish or even abusive
19. The anger of being falsely accused of doing something I didn't do
20. The anger of being falsely accused of being something I'm not
21. The anger and sadness of not being seen for who I am
22. The feeling of being invisible in a relationship
23. The feeling of being abused
24. The pressure of being a caretaker
25. The idea that living with an addict is normal or what I deserve
26. The anger of living or being with an addict
27. The belief that I'll never be enough

28. A parent telling me I'm defective in some way, making me less worthy of healthy love
29. The feeling of being desperate
30. The feeling that life is not fair
31. The shame of my body
32. Hatred toward another person for letting me down or not living up to expectations
33. The idea that everything is my fault all the time and I have to do better or suffer for it
34. The idea that anything that goes wrong is out of my control
35. The idea that karma is making life and love hard for me
36. What others say about me
37. The need for approval
38. The need to be liked
39. The need to be loved
40. The belief that I don't have a right to my feelings
41. The rules of association
42. The belief that if I show someone the real me, they'll leave
43. The feeling of discomfort that I had when I was a child or in a previous relationship
44. The anger of having something or someone forced on me
45. The feeling of guilt that comes from disappointing a parent or someone I love
46. The idea that I can't trust myself or another person
47. Being bullied
48. The embarrassment of growing up in a cult or having a family that wasn't "normal"
49. The anger of having to silence myself
50. The belief that I can't ever be the real me
51. The fear of self-expression
52. The idea that I'm never safe

53. The idea that I'll never get what I want
54. Convention
55. Other people's voices in my head, telling me what to do or who I should be
56. The time I got [insert . . .]
57. The sorrow of losing [insert . . .]
58. Not accomplishing my dream
59. Feeling like I don't have a right to an opinion or what I'm saying is dumb
60. The idea that what I think doesn't matter
61. The idea that money is the measure of success
62. The idea that money creates greed
63. The idea that I need someone else to take care of me and protect me, that I can't do it myself
64. The idea that I'm only here to take care of other people
65. The idea that I'm incapable of accomplishing anything
66. The idea that I can't have healthy love without struggle
67. The idea that I can't tell anyone what I'm really thinking
68. The idea that if I want to accomplish anything, I have to struggle
69. The idea that I need to conform to another person's wishes, desires, and expectations in order to be loved
70. The idea that I'm different in a negative way
71. The idea that no one will ever love me
72. The idea that everyone will love me like my wonderful father or mother did
73. The idea that I'm special and deserve to be treated that way
74. The idea that I have to give up on my own dreams and desires in order to be loved
75. The idea that I don't have anyone to help me or that asking for help is a sign of weakness
76. The idea that it's too late for me to find love

77. The idea that I don't matter
78. The idea that I'm the only one going through heartbreak in such a painful way
79. The idea that my destiny is to be sad
80. The idea that being alone is always a bad thing
81. The idea that I don't have any control over my situation
82. The idea that love is owed to me
83. The idea that the rules don't apply to me
84. The fear that there are no unseen helpers
85. The idea that people are inherently bad and will always seek to hurt me
86. The feeling of obligation to do what someone else says I should do
87. The feeling that I have to be perfect to be loved
88. The need to forgive everyone
89. The idea that I should take what I can get and be happy with it, even if it isn't what I want
90. The idea that settling for less is the right way to go
91. The resistance to whatever brings me joy
92. The reflex to be self-destructive or to self-sabotage
93. The fear of success
94. The fear of failure
95. The belief that happiness comes from outside of me
96. The idea that bad things are always my fault
97. The idea that I should always forgive others and let them back into my life, no questions asked
98. The need to control
99. The need to be controlled
100. The need to be friends with everyone, even if they don't have my best interests at heart

Letting Go Comprehensively Is Possible

When I began online dating—and dating again in general—in addition to letting go of the idea that I was too old to love and that I hadn't been on the dating scene since I was twenty-nine, there were other things I needed to let go of.

I hadn't considered my value on the open dating market for a very long time and didn't have a ton of confidence about how I'd stack up against the competition. It had also been a while since I truly cared about what men other than Hector thought of me, which meant I now had to bring my A game to market. This included dieting, exercising, and putting a certain priority on how I looked. But I didn't do it because I was trying to be something I wasn't, I was simply trying to be the best version of myself because I had a whole new level of profound love for myself. And to be honest, I could have stood to lose a few pounds.

I had to let go of the idea that by going out with someone else, I was actually cheating on Hector. And vice versa: that if he was out with someone else, he was actually cheating on me. Because we weren't together anymore. That was the truth of it all.

I had to let go of old reflexes that had me gravitate toward men who weren't great for me. Who didn't want what I wanted. Who didn't align with the options and end goal I'd set forth for myself.

I had to let go of the act of online dating itself, which felt weird and wonky and forced and stilted and plain old not right— like shopping for a life partner the same way I get books and makeup and yet another pair of yoga pants and, well, let's face it, everything on Amazon. I had to allow myself to sink into this new way of doing things as if it were the deepest, widest, plushest Barcalounger I'd ever had the privilege of resting my shrinking tushie in.

I had to make all of this stuff—every belief, sensation, and fear—my total and complete bitch. And I did that by letting go of it.

All of it.

And you know how I did it, right?

By relentlessly big wild loving myself, of course.

Chapter 9

THE PLAN

It took me ten years to carry out my "escape plan." One of the best parts about it was that I documented it in a lot of journals over the years. So when I was leaving my husband, I could just go through them and pull out what I'd needed in order to move ahead, clear about what needed to happen, how, and when. That plan was everything.

—Janice, 43, New Jersey

When I was sixteen, we had a holiday dinner and my aunt brought her famous homemade carrot cake for dessert. Since my mother was always monitoring my food intake, everybody got a piece but me. But I wanted some. And I was determined to get it.

So I made a plan. After everybody left, I waited patiently for my mom, dad, and brother to fall asleep, and then, at about two a.m., I tiptoed down into the kitchen. I flipped on the dim light over the stove so I could see what I was doing without attracting attention, took out the leftover carrot cake, and placed it ever so gently on the counter. Then I contemplated my strategy for digging in without anybody noticing at dinner the following night when my mom would surely re-serve it to my father and brother.

Not surprisingly, my mother was one step ahead of me. As I surveyed the cake structurally to determine where to cut, it appeared she had perfectly halved what was left, so she could tell if any little "mice" had nibbled at it while she wasn't looking.

You had to give it to her. She was good.

She had also swaddled the cake in so much tinfoil that it was difficult to unwrap without being noisy. Damn, the woman was a genius! If I hadn't been so aggravated with her and hungry, I might have actually been inspired. What she hadn't counted on, however, was that I was pretty smart myself. And up for the challenge. I was also highly motivated—and not just because my stomach was growling, but as a matter of pride. I would have some of that cake, dammit.

Determined, I gently opened the silverware drawer, grabbed a fork, and began poking away at the tinfoil's edges as if I were performing brain surgery . . . until I finally caught enough of the foil to pull at it easily with my thumb and forefinger. Then I slowly undressed the cake, careful not to move too quickly or loudly. Once I'd gotten all of the foil peeled off, preserving it in a way that would allow me to rewrap whatever was left after I'd had my due, I took a moment to wipe the sweat from my brow with the sleeve of my pajama top.

I surveyed the now fully exposed cake from various angles. How would I get at that perfect half-moon so no one would notice? It didn't take long to come to me: I'd turn the cake fully on its side and slice a thin piece from the bottom across the entire length so it would still be perfectly halved, just shorter. That would not only solve the problem but also yield me a generous portion.

Ha! She wasn't the only genius in the family!

Of course, the next morning, while my dad and I sat at the kitchen table for breakfast (one perfectly measured ounce of Raisin Bran in skim milk for me), she pulled the cake out of the freezer. I watched as she examined it with squinty eyes and a furrowed brow, even though I'd put it all back together as I found it rather nicely.

"Owen?" she said. "Does this cake look lower to you?"

My dad looked at me and tried not to burst out laughing.

"What do you mean? Looks the same as yesterday . . ."

Then he winked at me.

Data Makes the Case

I smile now when I think of that story, twisted as the situation was. And hey, I've evolved to a much better place. We all have, even my mother.

But it illustrates a point I'd like to make: this is how you survey your life. Without other people's input or approval, sometimes as an act of hunger and desperation in the middle of the night, while the world is asleep. It's up to you to figure out how to rise above and overcome the challenges that are presented to you on the way to achieving what you want—whether that's in life, love, or dessert.

And yet, as fulfilling as this sort of survey of ourselves may seem in theory, I know it can also feel scary in practice. After all, it's one thing to set goals and promise to love yourself forever, but it's another thing to actually do it.

But as I prepared to and then ultimately did let go those years ago, I was aided by something that was like the key to the city: a documented plan for change. Yep, I'd written down every-thing—my epiphany moment, my objective and end goals, how I'd get there, and what I needed to let go of . . . the whole shebang. This plan gave me the push, sometimes more than once, that I'd need to finally find my way home: to the happy, healthy piece of cake that, after a lifetime of searching, I finally believed I deserved.

And it is this push that will serve you, too, as you let go for love yourself.

In 1979, researchers at the Harvard Business School conducted a study on goal setting that had them analyze the graduating class to determine how many had set goals and had a plan for how they'd attain them.[31] Participants were asked a single question: Have you set written goals and created a plan for their attainment?

Eighty-four percent of the entire class had set no goals at all.

Thirteen percent had set written goals but had no concrete plans.

Three percent of the class had both written goals and con-crete plans.

Ten years later, the 13 percent of the class that had set writ-ten goals but had not created plans were making twice as much money as the 84 percent of the class that had set no goals at all. And the 3 percent of the class that had both written goals and a plan for achieving them were making ten times as much as the other 97 percent of the class.

More recently, researchers at Dominican University in Cali-fornia led a global study on goal setting with nearly 270 participants from all genders, walks of life, and cultural backgrounds.[32] They divided participants into groups according to who wrote down their goals and dreams and who didn't. The results showed that people who wrote down their goals and dreams on a regular basis were 42 percent more likely to achieve them than those who did not.

In "The Gender Gap and Goal Setting," a survey published in *Forbes*, CEO and author Mark Murphy found that people who vividly described their goals in written form (e.g., pictures, photos, drawings, etc.) were anywhere from 1.2 to 1.4 times more likely to succeed in accomplishing them than those who didn't.[33]

And a *USA Today* report on New Year's resolutions shows that people who write down their resolutions are more likely to keep them than people who simply think or talk about them— even if the only difference between these two groups of people is the act of writing their goals down beforehand.[34]

Given all of this data (and it's just the tip of the iceberg, there is so much more out there), it's clear that there's a case to be made for documenting your goals and creating a plan for meeting them. This is the push that puts people who succeed over the top.

And yet so few do it—actually write down their goals, let alone revise them.

The question is why?

In Murphy's gender gap survey, he found that only 20 percent of respondents wrote their goals down vividly enough that they could literally show them to other people and have them know exactly what they were trying to achieve.

As I see it, the problem can be the result of many factors. Some people may not be serious about their goals or want them badly enough. They may be too tired, overwhelmed, or defeated to do more work toward what they may see as an impossible dream. They may be fine with settling for the status quo, perfectly comfortable in a state of "it's not awful and it's not great." Perhaps they don't know how to get the things they want or believe that it's possible for them, so they give up trying for it. In these cases, documentation would just be a moot point.

Whichever of these things is keeping us from setting goals and creating a plan for reaching them, I stand firm in the hypothesis that it can all be laid at the feet of limiting beliefs—the conscious and subconscious mind battling for control over what comes next and whether we're to get it. Because writing down our goals and crafting a plan can be so powerfully effective, our limiting beliefs will do everything possible to discourage us from doing it, especially if it negates those beliefs or directly challenges them.

This can manifest in a variety of ways. Limiting beliefs can keep us too busy with what doesn't matter, or doesn't advance our cause, so we're unfocused on our goals and lack a plan for achieving them, and leave us too easily distracted by things like social media, the wrong relationships, and other people's dramas and motivations. These beliefs can hamstring us with tunnel vision or encourage us to focus on the wrong things, fearful of putting our ideas to paper, making them all too real . . . and us accountable.

Which conjures up a whole other set of issues: What if we fail at getting where we want to go? Or worse yet, what if we don't? What if we actually succeed at getting what we want and it's not the end-all-be-all we'd hoped for?

There it all is, in the format of our choosing, reminding us of what we wanted and how horribly wrong—or scarily right—it all went.

Then what?

This inner conflict happens at a level so deep that, just like our unacknowledged epiphanies, we're asleep to it. Which is why we can never stop being introspective. Writing down our plan and checking in with it daily will keep us honest and on the straight and narrow. We'll be headed in the direction of what we want while giving ourselves the fairest shot possible at getting it.

Storage, Encoding, and Linking Hemispheres

By now, you're probably seeing the choice here: corralling all the great work you've been doing into a documented plan for moving forward, or keeping it all loosey-goosey in your jam-packed brain, free to jostle about and get lost in translation or altogether.

If you're serious about having Big Wild Love, I strongly encourage you to do the former. Take this one final step for the win.

Because the scientific and anecdotal evidence is clear: the seemingly simple act of writing not only reinforces clarity of purpose and direction, but also unlocks all sorts of psychological dynamics that translate into real, tangible results, making the exercise well worth the time and effort.

Writing stuff down allows you to store information—on the computer, on paper, in your journal, etc.—and then retrieve it easily. This is critical, in that you must think about your end goal often if you want to successfully get there. Doing so inspires your subconscious mind to make it happen—to invite in the right people and opportunities, and deflect the rest.

For example, when I decided I wanted to give a TEDx talk, I thought about it constantly. I wrote down a game plan for getting there and steps I needed to take to be successful. As I prepared myself for the talk I hadn't yet been invited to give (by engaging a coach, writing and rewriting my talk, rehearsing it more than six hundred times in front of my two dogs and countless times in my mind), I was giving instructions to my subconscious: set me up for success.

I was so incredibly focused on giving this talk.

Then one morning, my coach sent me a link to an application for a TEDx event in my area. I had twenty-four hours to meet the deadline. *Seriously?* Not only that, but the application was robust and required me to not only be thoughtful, creative, and persuasive, but to also send in a video, which I did not have.

To make the situation even more complex, I had planned to spend that day and an overnight in New York City with friends and could not cancel for a variety of reasons.

Fortunately, I'd been gestating on this talk for months and was able to quickly write a short video script. Then I went out with friends, got back to the hotel at midnight, and did not sleep. Instead, I filled out the online application. I set my Microsoft Surface Pro on top of the hotel room Bible to give myself a better angle, and I hit record. You could see straight up my nostrils the whole time.

But I wanted it. And despite giving reviewers an up close and personal look at the inner workings of my nose, my passion and clarity showed. And, as you know, I got it.

I'm not saying this to brag or be a show-off, but rather to illustrate how the power of focus and intention influences the subconscious mind. And why writing stuff down and concentrating on it every minute you can works.

Writing down your goals and a plan for reaching them also allows you to "encode" the details.

I won't get into the technicalities since there's lots out there about encoding, other than saying that it's a biological process that allows you to remember things better when you write them down. And memory matters because it allows you to keep your end goal top of mind and your subconscious hard at work on your behalf.

It makes sense if you think about a time when you were in school and how you did best when you took notes in class and on the textbook. That's because reading alone would not have been enough for you to remember what you needed to know in order to pass the test on it or grasp the information. Writing things down makes them sticky.

This is also because of something called the "generation effect," which states that people demonstrate better memory for materials they've generated themselves than for material they've merely read.[35]

And lastly, writing things down allows your right and left brain hemispheres to work most effectively together. Author, speaker, and consultant Mary Morrissey states in an article on HuffPost.com: "If you just think about one of your goals or dreams, you're only using the right hemisphere of your brain, which is your imagination center. But if you think about something that you desire and then write it down, you also tap into the power of your logic-based left hemisphere."[36]

That, she says, sends your consciousness and every cell of your body a signal that says, "'I want this, and I mean it!'"

At a more basic level, writing things down encourages you to make daily progress in getting where you want to go because you have a clear place from which to move forward. Since your brain doesn't have to work so hard at remembering things, it's got more bandwidth for the task of processing information. And this, in turn, allows you to enjoy a higher level of thinking and more focused and purposeful action.

"I left my ex-husband clicking my heels and scared to death," says Kim, the forty-eight-year-old florist I introduced in chapter 4, who left her abusive marriage and alcoholic husband after twenty-seven years. "And yet I'd eventually gotten to a point where I knew who I was and what I was capable of because I'd put together a written plan for my life after leaving. I realized that you'd have to be out of your mind to try to leave a marriage, build a business, and raise daughters without one or knowing where you were headed."

When she'd had enough of life inside an unhappy relationship, Kim turned to a friend who'd been through her own challenging divorce and who had blazed the trail in creating a plan for leaving that had her not only surviving but also thriving in its aftermath. "She sat me down and told me exactly what I had to do, which included how to leave, address money issues, the house, everything.

   "She also helped me to see that I needed a plan for creating a new, more positive story for myself, one that talked about how my life would change for the better once I left."

   Kim talks about how much writing everything down helped. How being able to see her finances on the page in black and white and even the language she used to describe her life was powerful. "After I did it, I started talking to myself in a different way. Telling myself how I had to change my own narrative to believe that I was good and smart and capable and ambitious and talented and lovable . . . all the things I knew I was, but had forgotten for far too long. Creating that plan made all the difference!

   "Now, ten years later, I have a thriving business, thriving children, and yes, even love again. I'm in a really happy place."

Putting It All Together

Here's the good news: you've already started writing stuff down by following the exercises on these pages. You may be surprised at just how far along in this letting go process you are and how simple this step will be for you!

   In this step, we're going from theoretical to practical. You'll put together a plan you can use. First, you're going to incorporate all you've learned from moving through the previous five steps, creating a workable, usable, and dynamic plan of action.

Step #1

Decide how to capture your plan. We all have different systems for planning—some use a journal/planner, some use an Excel spreadsheet, some people plan in pictures and video, etc. I don't dare propose one way over the other. Instead, I'm going to recommend that deciding how and where you'll capture and track the plan and your activities *is* the first step. Select a method that feels best and most comfortable for *you*. It can be in a daily planner, a notebook, a three-ring binder, a series of folders, an artist's tablet, a big desk calendar, a white board, a vision board, a poster board, an Excel spreadsheet, a Word table/chart, etc. Heck, you can even get chalkboard paint or paper a wall in your house and do it up (I am personally in love with this idea and going to Home Depot for some paint when I finish writing this chapter!). For example, if you want to keep things private, then a journal or planner may be your best bet. If you're especially visual, go for the big board. See what I mean? Once you have your system in place, plan to review and track and update every week. I recognize that a daily review, while ideal, might be tough. And I want to make sure to set you up for success!

Step #2

Write down your epiphany and your objective. At the top of your [insert method], write down one or two succinct sentences that describe your epiphany moment. It's important to remember why you got started on this journey in the first place. Then encapsulate what you want in one or two sentences as an objective underneath. This is the big objective, and not the series of end goals you listed in chapter 5. Write it directly underneath the epiphany moment, so you can easily see both at a glance.

So, for example:

- **Epiphany:** He's never going to give me the commitment I want.
- **Objective:** A healthy, big wild loving partner who wants the committed, long-term relationship and marriage that I do and shares my timing and values.

I never want you to lose track of where you started, where you're going, and where you ultimately wind up because how you fill the space in between all of these things is what comes next.

Step #3

Build out your plan. Again, you can do it online or scribble it into a notepad or onto the chalkboard wall in your bedroom. You can use a chart or straight prose. Your call. Whatever you do, it should include the following elements because, again, you want to use them:

- **What I want.** This is where you present your several end goal(s).
- **How I'll get them.** This is where you lay out your options for getting to each end goal.
- **Action steps:** I recommend listing two to three actions you'll take to put each option into play.
- **When will I do these things?** You can reference this in terms of precise dates, weeks, or months. The point is to create a timeline that will keep you moving.
- **Results.** How will I measure my success? Once you know that, check in regularly with this plan to see and update your progress and identify whether some things need to be shifted, deleted, or changed altogether for bigger and more meaningful impact.

- **Notes:** Is there anything in particular you'd like to remember or capture that you think will be helpful or inform anything in the plan? If so, here's where to put it.

Since I like charts and find they're easy for at-a-glancing, here's an example of how I'd lay all of this out:

What I want (end goal)	How I'll get it (options)	Action steps	Timing	Results	Notes

If you use a chart, you could also color-code the columns and keep folders for each; that will give you a place to store any associated information (e.g., invites, notices, lists, e-mails, broader notes to yourself, etc.) so you don't bog down the chart with so much information it's unusable.

You could also lay your epiphany and end goal sentences on top of this chart so it would look like this:

EPIPHANY: He's never going to give me the commitment I want.

OBJECTIVE: A healthy, big wild loving partner who wants the committed, long-term relationship and marriage that I do and shares my timing and values.

What I want (end goal)	How I'll get it (options)	Action steps
A partner who wants what I do, which is marriage	• Fix-ups through friends • Online dating with a discerning eye	• Tell friends that I'm actively looking for someone who wants commitment • Register on dating sites that cater to the folks who are looking for more serious relationships versus casual flings • Engage with both

Again, it's your call as to how you want to do it. As you can see, there's a lot of leeway here regarding how you capture information and what you deem important. As long as you get it down somewhere so you can keep track and interact with it regularly, you're good. The intention will remain strong.

If you're writing all of this on a chalkboard wall, for example, you could also draw pictures of what that person looks like, or images associated with how it might make you feel (sunbursts, hearts, flowers, whatever). The more vivid your documentation (going back to the survey "The Gender Gap and Goal Setting"), the better!

Timing	Results	Notes
• By the end of the month	• Two fixups	• Liked first, not second; follow-up with friends if possible for more details
• By the end of the month	• Registered at three dating sites	
• Ongoing	• Currently talking with three prospects:	• Check email on sites once a day
	• Joe	• Dates scheduled
	• Dan	
	• Marcus	

The whole point of all of these steps is to keep things dynamic: easy to store, retrieve, track, and update. Life changes, approaches change, ideas and situations change, we change. Plans need to be dynamic. You'll want to keep this overview as tight as possible so you can look at it and revise as needed based on current circumstances. You also want to be able to look at it quickly and know what you need to do, whether it's getting done, how you can pick up the pace, whether you're on the right track, and as a way to remind you that you're doing great! Keep going!

Step #4

Lay out the obstacles and how you'll overcome them. What are the obstacles—perceived, current, or anticipated—that you could run into, and how do you plan to overcome them? Anticipate them and ways to rise above them before they even happen. Create a list of three obstacles and then then journal around the following prompts for each one.

- Is this possible?
- Is it probable?
  - If so, how can I solve it?
  - If not, provide the evidence.

If you feel there are more than three to contend with, go for it. I just don't want you to overwhelm yourself. Most importantly, I want you to feel prepared and energized around what you need to do.

I'm giving you a bit less structure and fewer examples for these exercises because (a) you should already have a lot of this work done and be able to pull content from your journals, and (b) it's really up to you to find your comfort zone with the system you'll use and the actual approach to getting it all down in one spot.

With that said, please resist the urge to copy what I've written as an example. Think it through. Use this as an opportunity to feel inspired and creative.

However you participate, know that there's always a way to get where you want to go. Even when the situation seems hopeless or less than ideal, you can do it. You just have to lay the problem on its side to see it from a new perspective, just like I did with that cake when I was a teenager. The answer will come to you. And I promise you, when it does, it will be as sweet as you can possibly imagine.

That's precisely what I did when I had that epiphany on that stranger's floor. I laid the problem on its side and finally saw it for what it was: I couldn't stay where I no longer belonged. I used my newfound sight to forge a different path. I did what I'm asking you to do—spent time in my feelings, figured out what I wanted, laid out my options, and created my list of letgoables, including self-deprivation.

And then, to solidify all that theoretical work, I wrote everything down into my own practical and comprehensive plan. That documentation did me proud. It kept me where I needed to be on my journey to love, especially when doubt and fear and momentary hunger—for what I'd lost or left behind or what simply wasn't good for me—risked my progress and everything I'd worked so hard to achieve.

When I was leaving Hector and our life together, along with everything else I'd known for two decades, I don't know how I would have done it without (a) Art of Pizza on speed dial, (b) the love and support of my family and friends, and (c) a documented plan for making my graceful exit and starting anew.

This documented plan kept me still when I felt like a spinning top. When fear and doubt pulled me into a swirling, hurling vortex of despair, the plan kept me from falling into the abyss.

When I was convinced that there was no way that I would survive the losses, that I was making the mistake of a lifetime in leaving Hector, when I wasn't sure my heart could withstand so much untethering, the plan reminded me I could.

It was there when I forgot why I was going and what I was planning. When I got lost in the details of moving, buying, selling, packing, job hunting, and resettling. When I was chewing my nails over money or gaining fifteen pounds from emotional binge-eating.

That plan set me straight: Stop eating, Jill. Stop chewing. Take a breath.

When I wondered whether I'd ever have sex again or date again or sleep again or come back and toss my head in flirty glee again.

That plan said yes. Have faith.

When I looked outward at a landscape that was being slowly, methodically, and sometimes excruciatingly uprooted. And then inward, at an inner life that was also being slowly, methodically, and sometimes excruciatingly transformed.

That plan reminded me who I was and why I deserved more than I had been willing to settle for.

It was, in the face of all of it, the one thing that held constant for almost a year of tumult, joy, sadness, excitement, terror, transition, and overhaul.

I kept journals.

Lists.

Charts.

Folders.

Advil.

Tissues.

Chips Ahoy!

I tracked everything in that plan. And when the reality of goodbye hit, I reached for it. Especially when I said goodbye to Hector. Sweet, good, kind, smart, charismatic, lovable, beautiful, and unavailable Hector . . .

He'd tried his best. We both had.

When I stood in front of that Toyota RAV4, determined and resolute and terrified, preparing for the fourteen-hour ride "home," with an overnight bag and my beautiful four-legged pup along for the ride.

When, despite my broken and palpitating heart, I realized I had no regrets.

That plan backed me up and said, "I got you, look ahead."

Without the plan, I might still be in that Chicago condo, living alone on the top floor of a three-flat, wondering how I got there and what time the pizza was coming.

But the plan took care of me. It was my sherpa, best friend, and champion. It allowed me to finish a process that had me question everything. That challenged me, validated me, forced me to look openly and honestly at myself, and ultimately showed me who was boss:

I was.

Without that plan—graspable, malleable, and waterproof (because it did wind up in the bathtub a few times)—I would not have what I have today:

Big Wild Love on all counts.

AFTERWORD

Then there was Dan. I met him on Match.com a year after leaving Hector and Chicago for good.

We had our first date at a restaurant in my new home of New Hope, Pennsylvania, for dinner. I got there early to collect my thoughts and get my bearings. After all, I'd been on enough dates at that point to know that I needed to manage my expectations and stay grounded in BWL.

Still, I had a weird feeling about this one. Dan stood out from the other guys I'd met online. In his e-mails and even on the few telephone conversations we'd had, he seemed more vulnerable and authentic. Even though he'd been married twice (which didn't scare me; to the contrary, I was compelled by his story as he was incredibly forthcoming), there was an innocence about him that intrigued me. He was a book willing to be opened. I liked that. I found it—and him—refreshing and curious and promising. After all, I was forty-two. Folks around my age had come from somewhere . . . I did too. Suffice to say, I was ready to meet him in the flesh.

As I sat there at a table for two, waiting, sipping seltzer water in my uniform of black jeans, a white T-shirt, and platform sandals, I couldn't help but wonder whether the hat I'd also decided to wear was too much. But only for a moment.

After all, the few friends I'd regaled with my stories of online dating egged me on. "You are rocking that hat," they said.

"Wear it," they dared.

So I did, and they were right. I loved myself, and I loved my fabulous bold hat.

It was a gift I'd bought for myself when I first moved back to the area: a pricey, slouchy, yellow straw fedora that tugged at my newly formed sense of empowerment. It wasn't your everyday baseball cap or simple wide-brim variety. There was something special in the way it was structured . . . wearing it not only had me exude courage and confidence, it made me feel bold and alive and pretty.

That hat screamed Big Wild Love.

I tipped it ever so slightly on my head and started to look outside the open windows that made up an entire wall of the front room, which spilled onto an outside patio. Keeping an eye out for him, I couldn't help but wonder: Would Dan be the one? Or would he be just a good night out? Or perhaps a rotten night out? I gave myself a few minutes to ruminate on these possibilities and then stopped myself, figuring I'd spent enough time holding myself to impossible expectations or guesstimating the future.

I looked over to the patio and saw him approaching the entrance, looking a bit lost, glancing into the restaurant to make sure he was in the right spot, a sign of relief registering on his face. This was the place, Karla's, a New Hope favorite. He made his way over.

Tall and handsome, he looked just like his picture—a perfect combination of Kurt Russell and Patrick Swayze. He wore blue jeans and a green Henley shirt, which was wrinkled like skin that had spent a whole month in the sun. Still, I liked it. It made me feel strangely safe. After all, a player would never show up for a date in anything less than pressed perfection.

"Jill?" he asked, putting out his hand as he walked toward me, dropping what looked like an old rain hat onto his chair.

Oh. My. God. He'd brought a hat! A weird hat. With a string for tying under your chin. It looked old and worn, like something that had been left for dead in a cubby in a mudroom after twenty years of rainstorms. I loved it in both a visceral and inexplicable way.

"Oh." He noticed me noticing his hat. "I brought it for you, they said it might rain . . ."

How sweet that he wanted to make sure to have something to keep me dry for walking to the car after dinner. But a hat? What about an umbrella? Wouldn't that have been a more obvious and less risky choice? After all, an old rain hat like his invited judgement or at least curiosity. It clearly had a story. What was it?

Between the hat and the shirt, I was absolutely beside myself. Dan was disruptive. And cute. And kind. Was I ready for that? For him?

I could tell he was in the same headspace, as he glanced up at my hat more than once with a look of what I interpreted as both confusion and horror. Did he find it offensive? Weird? Was he trying to figure out what it all meant too? Did he like me? Did I like him? Were we a match? Would he pass my test? Was his hat a test for me? Would we grow old together? Make each other our beneficiaries? Honeymoon in Hawaii or embark on an Alaskan cruise?

Take it easy, Jill, I remember thinking. *Calm yourself. BWL.* I repeated this several times to myself silently, in between our easy repartee and chemistry.

About midway through our meal, I noticed Dan reach into his pocket to turn off his phone, which was ringing, without even looking to see who it was. I intuited that as a good sign.

Still, despite all of the positives, I also knew that life could change on a dime and so too could this date. It could, in fact, have gone any number of ways, and I felt the fragility of it all.

Which reminded me of the night before I'd left Chicago for good, when Hector had come over to say goodbye. I remember thinking back then as well that this could go any number of ways. After all, was it really goodbye? We'd agreed, of course, to stay in touch and see how things went. He'd promised to visit me once I was settled. We even talked about keeping our relationship alive long-distance until he could comfortably retire from his state job with a full pension in five years. Only then could he think about moving. Five years. I don't think either one of us really believed it would happen. Or that he would ever choose me over friends, family, and a lifetime spent living in the Midwest.

What I did know was that, like my and Dan's date, there was a great deal of uncertainty and fragility in the air. On that last night, Hector could have begged me to stay. I could have begged him to leave. We could have begged each other to do any number of things.

But what actually happened didn't involve any begging at all. As we stood there in the center of my now disheveled apartment, cardboard boxes framing the once warm and inviting space like an old, tired canvas, we were awkward.

Until the time finally came for Hector to leave.

I remember thinking, *Now what?*

Would we hug it out and say, "See ya soon"? Or would there be a scene? Fighting. Crying. Name calling. Accusations. Things we'd held on to for more than a decade that would no longer stay down, like bad milk. Or perhaps we'd err on the side of melancholy.

There was really no way for me to predict how our last night in Chicago would end, other than falsely believing I'd already done my grieving. That I'd wrung all that emotion out like water from a towel once I'd made the gut-wrenching decision to let go.

But I was wrong. Because once Hector returned from taking Sophie for one last walk around my Lincoln Square city block, I went into a full Chernobyl meltdown.

The tears, the dry heaving, the sobbing, it just wouldn't stop. Hector pulled me close into his neck, and I proceeded to slowly cry my way down into his armpit, looking for a clean spot on his shirt to wipe my nose and working feverishly to take in every note of his scent. I wanted to memorize it, hold onto it for later, when I feared loneliness would set in and I'd need the familiarity and comfort. He'd been home for so long.

I sobbed out the words in staccato, between the nooks and crannies of my breath: "I don't want to live without you." Over and over again, like a mantra. As if repeating it until I was gasping for air would mean anything.

It took me about fifteen minutes to collect myself. At which point Hector put both hands on my shoulders and said this: "You don't have to live without me, Jilly. You don't."

Huh?

"Because in the end," he said, "whether we're together forever or not. That will be your choice."

This made no sense. I was the one who got to decide whether we'd be together forever? Was this him suddenly being prescient? I'd spent years trying to get him to choose me. Love me. Marry me. Promise me we'd have a lifetime together. And now he was telling me that whether that happened or not was up to me?

I had no idea what to do with that statement, so I dismissed it. I was emotionally and energetically spent. I'd also come too far in creating change to look back.

I was leaving. It didn't matter anymore.

Once I'd gone, I'd think back on those last words and scratch my head—especially when I was getting ready for bed at night in the early days of my move and, alone with Sophie, I wondered what Hector was doing. When I was browsing potential dates online, asking myself if I'd ever find love again. When I was walking down the hill into the quaint river town that sat at the base of the ski resort–turned townhouse community I now lived in, a far cry from the hustle and bustle of the city life.

But I learned something very valuable in all of that reflection: Hector was right.

It would be up to me. Whether to stay or let go. Whatever the situation was, it would always be my choice.

And now, sitting there with Dan, I was preparing myself for the next choice: whether or not this would be the guy. I studied him carefully as he shared the intimate details of his life while looking with soulful curiosity into my eyes.

Did Dan like me? I hoped so. But what had become more important, based on my newly empowered concept of choice, was whether I liked him. Whether I'd choose him, instead of whether he'd choose me. That was now the priority.

This would become the default for how I approached whatever I brought into my life—I had to be sure I wanted it. It had to be right for me first.

First.

Back in the days of Hector, I rarely stopped to contemplate my choices, let alone feel confident in the fact that I had them. This was, in hindsight, a large part of the problem. I was woefully disempowered. Instead of taking ownership of my own decisions, I let other people make them for me and took whatever happened as a result—the good and the bad—on the chin.

But not anymore. Big Wild Love changed all of that.

And you know what happened?

I not only found myself, but I got the guy too.

Keep reading.

After going through the process I've shared in this book, I learned to not only love myself but to keep doing it, no matter what. Oh sure, I have moments where I hate my menopausal belly and wish I had more money so I could hire people to cook vegetables for me, and I would love to know that someday I will fit back into the blue jeans I keep in an old chest in my bedroom because I just can't bring myself to get rid of them.

But . . . none of that stops me from smiling back at the mirror each morning and embracing the day with empowering beliefs in hand, knowing with certainty that I am worthy of all good things.

And on those days that I may struggle with old beliefs trying to wheedle their way back in, as can happen, especially in times of change, Big Wild Love keeps me honest. It reminds me to stay focused. It keeps me safe and grounded. Assures me in my darkest moments that my life is all right. Wonderful, even. That I've got this. That I can get through anything because I'm smart and strong and resilient and lovely, with fantastic imperfections (and a shoe collection to die for) that make me uniquely me. And I now have a key in my pocket that opens the door to letting go whenever I need to use it.

And yes, I do use it often, thank you very much. Because Big Wild Love also allows me to be human. Which is a very, very good thing.

Know what else happened as a result of my going through my own process? Not only did I wind up having a great date with Dan, turns out he had a great date with me, and another and another until we realized that we were in this for the long haul.

What made Dan even more special was that he not only loved me fully, but he also allowed me to love him fully in return, as evidenced by how comprehensively he brought me into his world, his story, and his heart. How he made me a priority. He even let me throw away his excessive number of Hawaiian shirts and any clothing item with a picture of a dragon on it (don't ask). He bought an iron.

Now that's love. Seriously.

I no longer had to hold back my feelings or worry about being too much for someone who didn't want all I had to offer. In allowing me to both give and receive love, he offered me the relationship I'd always wanted but could never grab onto. Until, that is, BWL and the six-step process transformed me. I finally learned that, among other things, there is a gift in everything, even heartbreak.

Together, they gave me the tools I needed to let go of Hector and Chicago, and the wherewithal to finally choose the *right* man for me. After just four dates, Dan and I moved in together, because when you're in your forties and have been through the six-step process, you don't need years to know if someone is "the one." Besides, you don't have that kind of time.

I certainly wasn't about to spend another decade in a relationship going nowhere. This time, I had picked the right guy for me, who was not only awesome, shared my interests, and was available, but who also wanted what I did from love.

We got married fourteen months after meeting, under a misty sky on the Delaware River with all of our friends and family in attendance—some of whom didn't believe it would happen. Frankly, neither did I. Which, as we all know by now, was precisely the problem.

Here's what else happened: Hector died. From cancer. Way

too young. At the time of his passing, we'd been apart for years. But it didn't matter. It was still painful. I cried for him every day for months in my car on the way to work. Even though I hadn't seen him much over the years.

Still, we remained friends from a distance, because we never lost the things that brought us together in the first place: love, honor, and respect. They just changed form. He was always the first person to call me on my birthday, which still meant something to me. We'd text, e-mail, and talk on the phone occasionally. The thing is, we did spend twelve years together, which at our ages was a pretty big chunk of our lives. And it was all good, save for his just not being able to give me the commitment and high priority in his life I'd wanted. Suffice to say, when he died, it was awful.

I grieved a lot. I still do sometimes, especially when I spend time with his friends and family, who are lovely and still very much part of my life. (Thank you, social media and Expedia.)

And yes, my husband grew to be fine with my residual feelings over Hector, but he wasn't at first. In the beginning, when we first learned of Hector's illness, Dan too had to move through his own process of Big Wild Love and letting go to be OK with the fact that his wife was grieving for another man.

The good news is the experience inspired him to move beyond his own feelings and limiting beliefs—the ones that told him people were either meant to be together or apart, there was nothing in between, and that I either loved him or Hector, but I couldn't love both—since he'd lost plenty at love prior to our union. He not only got on board with my crying but also came to understand love in a whole new way. That it doesn't have boundaries or definition. That it can take many forms and should. That just because you love someone romantically for a time, it doesn't mean that kind of love is meant to be forever. That it's not an either/or proposition—you either love them or hate them. That love, like energy, can shift and change. And that it's OK to let go in those moments, folks, when you decide it's just not right anymore. In fact, you must.

Besides, I remind my husband, I *married* him. When I'm sick and needy (because I'll admit that I can be both of these things in the face of a cold or flu or ache of any sort), or when we need to drive my parents to the airport at five a.m., Dan is there. And when he needs me to leave him alone in his man cave to meditate or play the guitar, or help him figure out what to wear for an important meeting at work (since ripped jeans and a T-shirt that says, "I Tame Lions" is rarely appropriate), I'm there. We do for each other the things husbands and wives do. Things I never did for Hector, and never would.

Although he doesn't really need me to remind him that I picked him anymore. Because we both honor Hector and the role he plays in our lives now that he's gone. He's become like a divine angel, important to us collectively in a weird and lovely sort of way.

Lastly, I'm happy. BWL and letting go have given me that.

I now know what to do with moments of stress. Let go. Love myself.

I know how to read the signs in my body that tell me something is right or wrong, or it's time to change. Let go. Love myself.

I know how to find my strength and have the hard conversations necessary to get me and someone I love—whether it's my husband, a girlfriend, or a family member—to a better place. Let go. Love myself.

I know when someone is worthy of my love and when they're not and what to do about both. Let go. Love myself.

I know what to do when I doubt who I am and whether what I've got is what I deserve. Let go. Love myself.

I know when my gut is telling me something that I wish it weren't that I should listen anyway. Let go. Love myself.

I know that I'll be OK because I've got myself—strong, resilient, kind, giving, and aging as gracefully as time, resources, and medical advancements will allow. Let go. Love myself.

I know that it was—and will continue to be—the sense of safety that stems from Big Wild Love that empowers me to move forward with boldness over and over again, as well as to let go and love myself.

I also know that it's always up to me to make my own choices and not leave that to other people or chance. I implore you to do the same. Every step in this book will ask you to make a choice— to choose yourself, practice BWL, and do the work even when it gets difficult, never stopping until you have the clarity you need to act on your own behalf, even if that clarity is at first painful. I am rooting for you the whole way through.

Let go. Love yourself. That's the road out.

Do this, and I promise you, whatever you have in your life that you don't want will either get better or go away entirely. I know this firsthand, which is not me saying I don't have any problems or wish I didn't need so much moisturizer or hate that my parents and all dogs won't be around forever. It's me saying it's all OK. I'm OK. I can always let go and love myself, which is almost as good as eating a box of Oreos at midnight with no aftereffects.

And yet I can't say that would be the case if I hadn't leaned into the power of Big Wild Love and letting go. Some days, I imagine what it would be like if everyone did it.

In fact, I imagine it a lot. Which is why I wrote this book. And got up and did that talk, on a day when I was clearly retaining water, in front of all of those cameras.

For you, my friend. I hope you'll work it hard. If you do, you'll go places you never imagined . . . in love and other areas of your life. Because the principles that lie within these pages are designed to set you up for success in all sorts of ways. They give you all the power. You just needed some gentle instruction on how and when to use it.

Don't we all.

You, too, can walk toward the love you always wanted—inside or outside your current relationship if you've got one, or by starting over if you don't. Possibility doesn't know age, gender, income, location, ethnicity, or circumstance. Your destiny is in your hands.

Use Big Wild Love as the ground beneath your feet. Pay attention to the signs that tell you change is in the offing. Let yourself see them and feel them with wild abandon; painful as they may be, resist the urge to go numb. Decide what you want and how you'll get it and then, despite your fear and heartbreak, let go. Over and over again. As often as you need, and however you need, until you're light enough to float on the magic carpet of self-love to better places.

Allow the love you have for yourself to lead you to the love that's possible with someone else. Use it to get the courage and confidence you need to make own your choices and take the risks inherent in letting go. And be comprehensive.

Make your plan and put it into action.

That's it. You can do it. You don't need a full bank account, another person, permission, forgiveness, closure, verve, a big personality, great legs, a lot of yoga pants, kitchen skills, bedroom skills, to love football, the gym, a weekend at the spa, or anything else you think you need—that's keeping you stuck—to make it happen.

You've got it all right now to let go for it, whatever "it" is for you. And I know you will.

NOTES

Introduction

1. Lea Rose Emery, "Too Many People Stay in Bad Relationships, New Survey Says, and Here's Why," *Bustle*, November 30, 2015, https://www.bustle.com/articles/126572-too-many-people-stay-in-bad-relationships-new-survey-says-and-heres-why.

2. "Bruce Lipton Quotes," BrainyQuote.com, BrainyMedia, Inc., accessed May 15, 2019, https://www.brainyquote.com/quotes/bruce_lipton_694102.

Chapter 1: Self-Love with Intention

3. "Love Sick: An Unhappy Marriage Can Be Hazardous to Your Health," Lifewise by Dr. Jan, LifeWise Inc., accessed June 21, 2019, https://www.drjananderson.com/love-sick-an-unhappy-marriage-can-be-hazardous-to-your-health/.

Chapter 2: The Story You Tell Yourself

4. Peter Halligan, quoted in Alok Jha, "Where belief is born," *The Guardian*, July 29, 2005, https://www.theguardian.com/science/2005/jul/29/psychology.guardianweekly.

5. Daniel T. Gilbert, Romin W. Tafarodi, and Patrick S. Malone, "You Can't Not Believe Everything You Read," *Journal of Personality and Social Psychology* 65, no. 2 (August 1993): 221–33, http://dx.*doi*.org/10.1037/0022-3514.65.2.221.

6. Ibid.

7. Annie Duke, "Why Your Brain Clings to False Beliefs (Even When It Knows Better)," *Fast Company*, February 11, 2018, https://www.fastcompany.com/40528587/why-your-brain-clings-to-false-beliefs-even-when-it-knows-better.

8. Nick Skillicorn, "Evidence that children become less creative over time (and how to fix it)," Idea to Value, August 5, 2016, https://www.ideatovalue.com/crea/nickskillicorn/2016/08/evidence-children-become-less-creative-time-fix/.

9. Matt Sandrini, "Limiting beliefs: The science behind thoughts that hold you back," Time Zillionaire, November 24, 2016, https://www.timezillionaire.com/limiting-beliefs/.

10. Bruce H. Lipton, *The Biology of Belief: Unleashing the Power of Consciousness, Matter, & Miracles* (Carlsbad, CA: Hay House, 2008), 141.

Chapter 3: New Beliefs in Practice

11. Benjamin Hardy, "To Have What You Want, You Must Give Up What's Holding You Back," Mission.org, Medium, June 9, 2018.

Chapter 4: The Epiphany

12. Elise Ballard, *Epiphany: True Stories of Sudden Insight to Inspire, Encourage, and Transform* (New York: Harmony Books, 2011), 2–4.

13. Wei James Chen and Ian Krajbich, "Computational Modeling of Epiphany Learning," *Proceedings of the National Academy of Sciences of the United States of America* 114,

no. 18 (May 2017): 4637–42, https://doi.org/10.1073/pnas.1618161114.

Chapter 5: The Aftermath

14. Olivia Foster, "Is sleeping with someone else the best way to move on? New study shows more than half of people rebound from their former partners in just one month," *Daily Mail*, November 17, 2014, https://www.dailymail.co.uk/femail/article-2834921/New-study-shows-half-people-rebound-former-partners-just-one-month.html.

15. Claudia C. Brumbaugh and R. Chris Fraley, "Too fast, too soon? An empirical investigation into rebound relationships," *Journal of Social and Personal Relationships* 32, no. 1 (2014): 99–118, https://doi.org/10.1177/0265407514525086.

16. Lauren Vinopal, "5 Things That Happen to Your Emotions When You Bottle Them Up," Fatherly, June 4, 2018, https://www.fatherly.com/health-science/health-risks-holding-back-emotions/.

17. Deborah Smith, "Angry thoughts, at-risk hearts," *American Psychological Association* 34, no. 3 (March 2003): 46, https://www.apa.org/monitor/mar03/angrythoughts.

18. Adam Cohen, "Research on the Science of Forgiveness: An Annotated Bibliography," *Greater Good*, October 1, 2004, https://greatergood.berkeley.edu/article/item/the_science_of_forgiveness_an_annotated_bibliography.

19. C. Sue Carter and Stephen W. Porges, "The biochemistry of love: An oxytocin hypothesis," *EMBO Reports* 14, no. 1 (January 2013): 12–16, https://doi.org/10.1038/embor.2012.191.

20. George Dvorsky, "The Best Way to Recover from a Break-Up—According to Science," *Daily Explainer*, February 10, 2015, https://io9.gizmodo.com/the-best-way-to-recover-from-a-break-up-according-to-1684775462.

21. Gary W. Lewandowski Jr., "Promoting positive emotions following a relationship dissolution through writing," *The Journal of Positive Psychology* 4, no. 1 (January 2009): 21–31, https://doi.org/10.1080/17439760802068480.

Chapter 6: The End Goal

22. Dan Slater, quoted in Aziz Ansari, *Modern Romance* (New York: Penguin, 2015), 96. https://www.amazon.com/Love-Time-Algorithms-Technology-Meeting-ebook/dp/B008EKMDWG

23. Tracey Carr, "The Importance of Knowing What You Want," The Glasshammer, accessed May 15, 2019, https://theglasshammer.com/2017/03/22/importance-knowing-want/.

Chapter 7: The Options

24. Jonathan D. D'Angelo and Catalina L. Toma, "There Are Plenty of Fish in the Sea: The Effects of Choice Overload and Reversibility on Online Daters' Satisfaction with Selected Partners, *Media Psychology* 20, no. 1 (2017): 1–27, https://doi.org/10.1080/15213269.2015.1121827.

25. A.W. Geiger and Gretchen Livingston, "8 facts about love and marriage in America," Fact Tank, Pew Research Center, February 13, 2019, https://www.pewresearch.org/fact-tank/2019/02/13/8-facts-about-love-and-marriage/.

26. Isabel Thottam, "10 Online Dating Statistics You Should Know," eharmony.com, accessed May 15, 2019, https://www.eharmony.com/online-dating-statistics/.

27. Aaron Smith and Monica Anderson, "5 facts about online dating," Fact Tank, Pew Research Center, February 29, 2016, https://www.pewresearch.org/fact-tank/2016/02/29/5-facts-about-online-dating/.

28. Barry Schwartz, "More Isn't Always Better," *Harvard Business Review*, June 2006, https://hbr.org/2006/06/more-isnt-always-better.

29. Shankha Basu and Krishna Savani, "To Make Better Choices, Look at All Your Options Together," *Harvard Business Review Online*, June 28, 2017, https://hbr.org/2017/06/to-make-better-choices-look-at-all-your-options-together.

Chapter 8: The Letting Go Hit List

30. Geoffrey James, "Sitting Near a Multitasker Decreases Your Intelligence by 17 Percent," Inc.com, August 24, 2018, https://www.inc.com/geoffrey-james/multitasking-reduces-your-intelligence-by-17.html.

Chapter 9: The Plan

31. Annabel Acton, "How to Set Goals (And Why You Should Write Them Down)," Forbes.com, November 3, 2017, https://www.forbes.com/sites/annabelacton/2017/11/03/how-to-set-goals-and-why-you-should-do-it/#3840a272162d.

32. Mary Morrissey, "The Power of Writing Down Your Goals and Dreams," HuffPost, September 14, 2016, updated December 6, 2017, https://www.huffpost.com/entry/the-power-of-writing-down_b_12002348.

33. Mark Murphy, "Neuroscience Explains Why You Need to Write Down Your Goals If You Actually Want to Achieve Them," Forbes.com, April 15, 2018, https://www.forbes.com/sites/markmurphy/2018/04/15/neuroscience-explains-why-you-need-to-write-down-your-goals-if-you-actually-want-to-achieve-them/#2e443f887905.

34. Nabin Paudyal, "Here's Why Writing Down Your Goals Really Does Work," Lifehack, accessed May 15, 2019, https://

www.lifehack.org/385087/heres-why-writing-down-your-goals-really-does-work.

35. Murphy, "Neuroscience Explains Why You Need to Write Down Your Goals."

36. Morrissey, "The Power of Writing Down Your Goals and Dreams."

ACKNOWLEDGMENTS

Thank you . . .

Agent Elizabeth Kracht, editor Neil Gordon, and editor/gal pal/adopted sister Joy Stocke, for not only completing me, guiding me, inspiring me, championing me, and grounding me, but making me a better writer and human. You are *the* trifecta. The inner sanctum without whom this book would still be a twinkle in my eye.

Ajit Matthew George. A universe full of gratitude for seeing me and my message. The shot you gave me on the TEDx Wilmington stage was a game changer.

TEDx sisters who shared the day with me and have since become treasured friends, role models, and mentors. You show me what it means to be vibrant and resilient at any age. I'm talking to you, Lu Ann Cahn and Diane V. Capaldi. And, of course, Susan Sandler, without whom I'd still be scratching my head on message and so much more. We were meant to travel this path of reinvention together.

My fellow gingers. Illona Kimberly Nagy, for helping me sculpt my pile of clay into something special. And Denise Donnelly

Petti, for not only giving me digital presence, but steadying the emotional vine whenever I swung just a little too hard.

Dr. Suzana Flores, my TEDx sister, agent sister, and adopted life sister, for being so smart, courageous, and generous with both your knowledge and your friendship. I'm so glad life brought us together.

Patty Cara, for answering my texts when it counted most . . . knowing I have your uber-creative brain on speed dial keeps me out of the pizza parlor.

Jess Rinker, for lighting the path with your immense talent, your unwavering support, and your adorable cortisol-lowering puppy.

Michelle Proudfoot Virirakis and Christine Passarelli—sisterhood of the black stretch pants—for listening, cheerleading, and always being on the back deck (virtual and otherwise) when I need you.

Big sisters Joan Cantwell and Marilyn Soltis, for being there from the start, always one step ahead of me, readying me for what comes next, rooting for my success. We found our BWL together, didn't we?

My bestie, Deb Weissberg. For role-modeling BWL in practice. And for always being there, no matter what, to help me let go.

She Writes Press publisher Brooke Warner, Crystal Patriarche at BookSparks, and your amazingly brilliant, pioneering, award-winning, industry-disrupting, fearless, badass, community-building, world-rocking teams. For everything, including the sisterhood you've built and the access you've provided. You give your authors literary life and *lift*, and I'm honored to be on this magic carpet ride with you.

Hector. Sweet Hector, who taught me how much BWL mattered. I know you're watching, and I feel you around me often. See you again someday . . .

My wonderfully supportive and giving parents, who always told me I could, even when it was hard. When I would ask, "What if I fail?" you would say, "What if you succeed?" I would not have had the courage to find my own BWL or write this book without you.

And Dan. That hat. That wrinkled shirt. That look of confusion. It all had me at hello. You have the biggest heart, gentlest spirit, and most special soul of anyone I've ever known. Thank you for being the ground under my feet while I brought the dream of this book to life. You're my earth, my inspiration, and the meaning of Big Wild Love in the dictionary of my heart.

ABOUT THE AUTHOR

Jill Sherer Murray is a TEDx speaker, author, influencer, blogger, coach, and the founder of Let Go For It, a lifestyle brand dedicated to helping individuals and businesses let go for a better life and results. She is also an award-winning journalist and communications leader who can trace practically every success she's had in her career, love life, and more to letting go.

Her TEDx talk, "The Unstoppable Power of Letting Go," has been viewed by millions.

Murray spent a year studying improvisational comedy at the famous Second City Training Center in Chicago, and another five years writing a popular blog called "Diary of a Writer in Midlife Crisis" for Wild River Review. She also let go of just about everything to put her weight in *Shape* magazine—twelve times—as part of a yearlong assignment to document her weight loss journey for millions of readers. You can learn more about her at www.letgoforit.com.

SELECTED TITLES FROM SHE WRITES PRESS

She Writes Press is an independent publishing company founded to serve women writers everywhere. Visit us at www.shewritespress.com.

Letting Go into Perfect Love: Discovering the Extraordinary After Abuse by Gwendolyn M. Plano. $16.95, 978-1-938314-74-2. After staying in an abusive marriage for twenty-five years, Gwen Plano finally broke free—and started down the long road toward healing.

Note to Self: A Seven-Step Path to Gratitude and Growth by Laurie Buchanan. $16.95, 978-1-63152-113-3. Transforming intention into action, *Note to Self* equips you to shed your baggage, bridging the gap between where you are and where you want to be—body, mind, and spirit—and empowering you to step into joy-filled living *now*.

Stop Giving it Away: How to Stop Self-Sacrificing and Start Claiming Your Space, Power, and Happiness by Cherilynn Veland. $16.95, 978-1-63152-958-0. An empowering guide designed to help women break free from the trappings of the needs, wants, and whims of other people—and the self-imposed limitations that are keeping them from happiness.

Loveyoubye: Holding Fast, Letting Go, And Then There's The Dog by Rossandra White. $16.95, 978-1-938314-50-6. A soul-searching memoir detailing the painful, but ultimately liberating, disintegration of a twenty-five-year marriage.

Learning to Eat Along the Way by Margaret Bendet. $16.95, 978-1-63152-997-9. After interviewing an Indian holy man, newspaper reporter Margaret Bendet follows him in pursuit of enlightenment and ends up facing demons that were inside her all along.

Say It Out Loud: Revealing and Healing the Scars of Sexual Abuse by Roberta Dolan. $16.95, 978-1-938314-99-5. An in-depth guide to healing the wounds caused by sexual abuse, written by a survivor who's lived the process firsthand.